Official

SQA Past Papers

WITH ANSWERS

Higher
Human Biology

2010–2014

D1438241

HODDER
GIBSON
AN HACHETTE UK COMPANY

Hodder Gibson is grateful to the copyright holders, as credited on the final page of the Question Section, for permission to use their material. Every effort has been made to trace the copyright holders and to obtain their permission for the use of copyright material. Hodder Gibson will be happy to receive information allowing us to rectify any error or omission in future editions.

Hachette UK's policy is to use papers that are natural, renewable and recyclable products and made from wood grown in sustainable forests. The logging and manufacturing processes are expected to conform to the environmental regulations of the country of origin.

Orders: please contact Bookpoint Ltd, 130 Park Drive, Abingdon, Oxon OX14 4SE. Telephone: (44) 01235 827720. Fax: (44) 01235 400454.

Lines are open 9.00–5.00, Monday to Saturday, with a 24-hour message answering service. Visit our website at www.hoddereducation.co.uk. Hodder Gibson can be contacted direct on: Tel: 0141 848 1609; Fax: 0141 889 6315; email: hoddergibson@hodder.co.uk

This collection first published in 2014 by

Hodder Gibson, an imprint of Hodder Education,

An Hachette UK Company

2a Christie Street

Paisley PA1 1NB

¡BrightRED   Hodder Gibson is grateful to Bright Red Publishing Ltd for collaborative work in preparation of this book and all PUBLISHING SQA Past Paper, National 5 and Higher for CfE Model Paper titles 2014.

Typeset by PDQ Digital Media Solutions Ltd, Bungay, Suffolk NR35 1BY

Printed in the UK

A catalogue record for this title is available from the British Library

ISBN 978-1-4718-3684-8

3 2 1

2015 2014

Introduction

Study Skills – what you need to know to pass exams!

Pause for thought

Many students might skip quickly through a page like this. After all, we all know how to revise. Do you really though?

Think about this:

"IF YOU ALWAYS DO WHAT YOU ALWAYS DO, YOU WILL ALWAYS GET WHAT YOU HAVE ALWAYS GOT."

Do you like the grades you get? Do you want to do better? If you get full marks in your assessment, then that's great! Change nothing! This section is just to help you get that little bit better than you already are.

There are two main parts to the advice on offer here. The first part highlights fairly obvious things but which are also very important. The second part makes suggestions about revision that you might not have thought about but which WILL help you.

Part 1

DOH! It's so obvious but …

Start revising in good time

Don't leave it until the last minute – this will make you panic.

Make a revision timetable that sets out work time AND play time.

Sleep and eat!

Obvious really, and very helpful. Avoid arguments or stressful things too – even games that wind you up. You need to be fit, awake and focused!

Know your place!

Make sure you know exactly **WHEN and WHERE** your exams are.

Know your enemy!

Make sure you know what to expect in the exam.

How is the paper structured?

How much time is there for each question?

What types of question are involved?

Which topics seem to come up time and time again?

Which topics are your strongest and which are your weakest?

Are all topics compulsory or are there choices?

Learn by DOING!

There is no substitute for past papers and practice papers – they are simply essential! Tackling this collection of papers and answers is exactly the right thing to be doing as your exams approach.

Part 2

People learn in different ways. Some like low light, some bright. Some like early morning, some like evening / night. Some prefer warm, some prefer cold. But everyone uses their BRAIN and the brain works when it is active. Passive learning – sitting gazing at notes – is the most INEFFICIENT way to learn anything. Below you will find tips and ideas for making your revision more effective and maybe even more enjoyable. What follows gets your brain active, and active learning works!

Activity 1 – Stop and review

Step 1

When you have done no more than 5 minutes of revision reading STOP!

Step 2

Write a heading in your own words which sums up the topic you have been revising.

Step 3

Write a summary of what you have revised in no more than two sentences. Don't fool yourself by saying, "I know it, but I cannot put it into words". That just means you don't know it well enough. If you cannot write your summary, revise that section again, knowing that you must write a summary at the end of it. Many of you will have notebooks full of blue/black ink writing. Many of the pages will not be especially attractive or memorable so try to liven them up a bit with colour as you are reviewing and rewriting. **This is a great memory aid, and memory is the most important thing.**

Activity 2 — Use technology!

Why should everything be written down? Have you thought about "mental" maps, diagrams, cartoons and colour to help you learn? And rather than write down notes, why not record your revision material?

What about having a text message revision session with friends? Keep in touch with them to find out how and what they are revising and share ideas and questions.

Why not make a video diary where you tell the camera what you are doing, what you think you have learned and what you still have to do? No one has to see or hear it, but the process of having to organise your thoughts in a formal way to explain something is a very important learning practice.

Be sure to make use of electronic files. You could begin to summarise your class notes. Your typing might be slow, but it will get faster and the typed notes will be easier to read than the scribbles in your class notes. Try to add different fonts and colours to make your work stand out. You can easily Google relevant pictures, cartoons and diagrams which you can copy and paste to make your work more attractive and **MEMORABLE**.

Activity 3 – This is it. Do this and you will know lots!

Step 1

In this task you must be very honest with yourself! Find the SQA syllabus for your subject (www.sqa.org.uk). Look at how it is broken down into main topics called MANDATORY knowledge. That means stuff you MUST know.

Step 2

BEFORE you do ANY revision on this topic, write a list of everything that you already know about the subject. It might be quite a long list but you only need to write it once. It shows you all the information that is already in your long-term memory so you know what parts you do not need to revise!

Step 3

Pick a chapter or section from your book or revision notes. Choose a fairly large section or a whole chapter to get the most out of this activity.

With a buddy, use Skype, Facetime, Twitter or any other communication you have, to play the game "If this is the answer, what is the question?". For example, if you are revising Geography and the answer you provide is "meander", your buddy would have to make up a question like "What is the word that describes a feature of a river where it flows slowly and bends often from side to side?".

Make up 10 "answers" based on the content of the chapter or section you are using. Give this to your buddy to solve while you solve theirs.

Step 4

Construct a wordsearch of at least 10 X 10 squares. You can make it as big as you like but keep it realistic. Work together with a group of friends. Many apps allow you to make wordsearch puzzles online. The words and phrases can go in any direction and phrases can be split. Your puzzle must only contain facts linked to the topic you are revising. Your task is to find 10 bits of information to hide in your puzzle, but you must not repeat information that you used in Step 3. DO NOT show where the words are. Fill up empty squares with random letters. Remember to keep a note of where your answers are hidden but do not show your friends. When you have a complete puzzle, exchange it with a friend to solve each other's puzzle.

Step 5

Now make up 10 questions (not "answers" this time) based on the same chapter used in the previous two tasks. Again, you must find NEW information that you have not yet used. Now it's getting hard to find that new information! Again, give your questions to a friend to answer.

Step 6

As you have been doing the puzzles, your brain has been actively searching for new information. Now write a NEW LIST that contains only the new information you have discovered when doing the puzzles. Your new list is the one to look at repeatedly for short bursts over the next few days. Try to remember more and more of it without looking at it. After a few days, you should be able to add words from your second list to your first list as you increase the information in your long-term memory.

FINALLY! Be inspired...

Make a list of different revision ideas and beside each one write **THINGS I HAVE** tried, **THINGS I WILL** try and **THINGS I MIGHT** try. Don't be scared of trying something new.

And remember – "FAIL TO PREPARE AND PREPARE TO FAIL!"

Higher Human Biology

The exam

The Higher Human Biology exam has three sections. Each year, Section A, consisting of multiple choice questions, is done best by candidates while Section C, containing the extended response questions, is done least well. This is partly because of the relative demand of the questions, but also because the majority of candidates leave Section C until last when they are tired and perhaps running out of time. A strategy you could adopt would be to attempt at least one of the extended response questions at the start of the exam.

The exam contains around 30% of more demanding "A-type" questions. These questions often require two linked pieces of knowledge or contain two problem solving steps to complete, so are more challenging. They often start with words like "explain" or "suggest". These questions are mixed amongst more straightforward "C-type" questions, throughout the first two sections of the exam. "C-type" questions often start with words like "name" or "state". A strategy you could adopt would be to firstly focus on all of the "C-type" questions in the paper before spending more time thinking about the "A-type" questions. This strategy should ensure that you score the most marks that you possibly can.

Section A – multiple choice questions

When examiners write the multiple choice questions, they use their experience to identify the most common errors candidates tend to make and then they place these errors as alternative answers within the question. This means that when looking at the four answers to a multiple choice question, the alternative answers are well designed to distract candidates from the correct answer. A strategy you could adopt to avoid distraction is to cover up the four alternative answers before attempting the question. Hopefully, the answer you then decide on is one of the options you have covered up!

When you cannot use this strategy, there is a second strategy you can adopt. This time you should look at all the answers in turn and eliminate those that are clearly wrong. Hopefully, this will allow you to arrive at the correct answer or at least increase your chances of guessing the correct answer.

Section B – short answer questions

This section contains the majority of the marks in the paper and contains questions from all three Units of the course and at least two large problem solving-based questions.

When using these past papers, you should identify Section B questions, on the topic you have been studying, from different papers. Aim to complete the first question and then check your answers. Revise aspects you need to before attempting the second question and so on. This strategy should ensure that your knowledge of the topic is good enough to pass any question relating to it that appears in the exam.

It is also a good strategy to not attempt any questions in one paper until you have completed the course and are getting close to the exam. You should then attempt this paper in its entirety. This is a good way of identifying topics you need to focus on in the last few days prior to the exam.

A common error candidates make is not reading the question properly. For example, there is always one question in Section B where you have to either add a label or an arrow to a diagram. Candidates often do not answer this straightforward question, as no space is present for an answer. A strategy that you could use to avoid this is to read each question twice and the second time underline the term that describes the task to be done. This works particularly well when distinguishing "describe" from "explain" questions. Candidates often muddle these terms up. It should be noted that describe questions often require the use of information or data already provided in the question, while explain questions always require application of knowledge.

Problem solving questions

Candidates are generally better at handling problem solving questions. It is worth making sure that you can draw line or bar graphs, read graphs and carry out percentage calculations. These skills are always assessed. Check after taking a straightforward reading from a graph that the units are given in the answer space. If not, then you must enter these to gain the mark. You should also practise taking readings from graphs with two vertical axes.

There will always be a practical-based question in the paper. Make sure that you can identify variables which should remain constant during the investigation. In a laboratory experiment, concentrations and volumes should be considered while in other investigations human or environmental variables should be considered. Conclusions drawn must relate to the aims of the investigation and not simply restate experimental results.

Section C – extended response questions

This section contains two "essay" type questions. The first question is structured for you, so you simply have to write your answer under each heading. Remember that if the question section is worth four marks then the examiners are looking for at least four separate points on the topic. Do not add diagrams unless they illustrate something you have not already described. All diagrams must be clearly labelled or marks will not be awarded for them.

The second question is unstructured and you should structure this yourself by entering relevant subheadings. The use of bullet points will cost you a coherence mark here, so try to write paragraphs containing linked sentences. Try to be concise. If you write too much you are liable to have given irrelevant information and this will cost you a mark.

Good luck!

Remember that the rewards for passing Higher Human Biology are well worth it! Your pass will help you get the future you want for yourself. In the exam, be confident in your own ability. If you are not sure how to answer a question, trust your instincts and just give it a go anyway – keep calm and don't panic! GOOD LUCK!

HIGHER

2010

[BLANK PAGE]

FOR OFFICIAL USE

Total for
Sections B & C

X009/301

NATIONAL
QUALIFICATIONS
2010

THURSDAY, 27 MAY
1.00 PM – 3.30 PM

HUMAN BIOLOGY
HIGHER

Fill in these boxes and read what is printed below.

Full name of centre

Town

Forename(s)

Surname

Date of birth

Day   Month   Year   Scottish candidate number

Number of seat

SECTION A—(30 marks)

Instructions for completion of Section A are given on page two.

For this section of the examination you must use an **HB pencil**.

SECTIONS B AND C—(100 marks)

1 (a) All questions should be attempted.

  (b) It should be noted that in **Section C** questions 1 and 2 each contain a choice.

2 The questions may be answered in any order but all answers are to be written in the spaces provided in this answer book, **and must be written clearly and legibly in ink**.

3 Additional space for answers will be found at the end of the book. If further space is required, supplementary sheets may be obtained from the Invigilator and should be inserted inside the **front** cover of this book.

4 The numbers of questions must be clearly inserted with any answers written in the additional space.

5 Rough work, if any should be necessary, should be written in this book and then scored through when the fair copy has been written. If further space is required a supplementary sheet for rough work may be obtained from the Invigilator.

6 Before leaving the examination room you must give this book to the Invigilator. If you do not, you may lose all the marks for this paper.

Read carefully

1   Check that the answer sheet provided is for **Human Biology Higher (Section A)**.

2   For this section of the examination you must use an **HB pencil**, and where necessary, an eraser.

3   Check that the answer sheet you have been given has **your name**, **date of birth**, **SCN** (Scottish Candidate Number) and **Centre Name** printed on it.

     Do not change any of these details.

4   If any of this information is wrong, tell the Invigilator immediately.

5   If this information is correct, **print** your name and seat number in the boxes provided.

6   The answer to each question is **either** A, B, C or D. Decide what your answer is, then, using your pencil, put a horizontal line in the space provided (see sample question below).

7   There is **only one correct** answer to each question.

8   Any rough working should be done on the question paper or the rough working sheet, **not** on your answer sheet.

9   At the end of the examination, put the **answer sheet for Section A inside the front cover of this answer book**.

Sample Question

The digestive enzyme pepsin is most active in the

A   stomach

B   mouth

C   duodenum

D   pancreas.

The correct answer is **A**—stomach. The answer **A** has been clearly marked in **pencil** with a horizontal line (see below).

Changing an answer

If you decide to change your answer, carefully erase your first answer and, using your pencil, fill in the answer you want. The answer below has been changed to **D**.

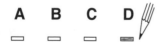

SECTION A

All questions in this section should be attempted.

Answers should be given on the separate answer sheet provided.

1. The diagram below shows an enzyme-catalysed reaction taking place in the presence of an inhibitor.

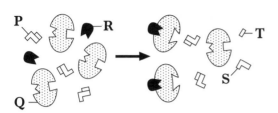

Which line in the table below identifies correctly the molecules in the reaction?

	Inhibitor	Substrate	Product
A	P	R	S
B	Q	P	S
C	R	P	T
D	R	Q	T

2. The following diagram shows a branched metabolic pathway.

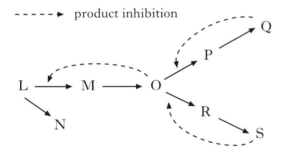

Which reaction would tend to occur if both Q and S are present in the cell in high concentrations?

A   L → M

B   R → S

C   O → P

D   L → N

3. A fragment of DNA was found to have 120 guanine bases and 60 adenine bases. What is the total number of sugar molecules in this fragment?

A   60

B   90

C   180

D   360

4. The following information refers to protein synthesis.

tRNA anticodon	amino acid carried by tRNA
G U G	Histidine (his)
C G U	Alanine (ala)
G C A	Arginine (arg)
A U G	Tyrosine (tyr)
U A C	Methionine (met)
U G U	Threonine (thr)

What order of amino acids would be synthesised from the base sequence of DNA shown?

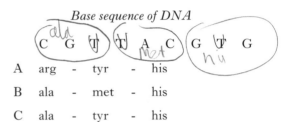

Base sequence of DNA

C G T   T A C   G T G

A   arg - tyr - his

B   ala - met - his

C   ala - tyr - his

D   arg - tyr - thr

5. In which of the following is the cell organelle listed correctly with its function?

	Cell organelle	Function
A	Mitochondrion	Anaerobic respiration
B	Ribosome	Release of ATP
C	Lysosome	Synthesis of enzymes
D	Nucleolus	Synthesis of RNA

6. Carrier molecules involved in the process of active transport are made of

A   protein

B   carbohydrate

C   lipid

D   phospholipid.

[Turn over

7. An investigation was carried out into the uptake of sodium ions by animal cells. The graph shows the rates of sodium ion uptake and breakdown of glucose at different concentrations of oxygen.

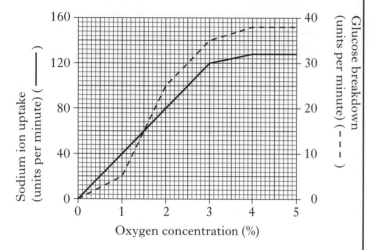

Calculate the number of units of sodium ions that are taken up over a 5 minute period when the concentration of oxygen in solution is 2%.

A   80

B   100

C   400

D   500

8. Which of the following statements about viruses is true?

A   Viral protein directs the synthesis of new viruses.

B   New viruses are assembled outside the host cell.

C   Viral protein is injected into the host cell.

D   Viral DNA directs the synthesis of new viruses.

9. What is the significance of chiasma formation?

A   It results in the halving of the chromosome number.

B   It results in the pairing of homologous chromosomes.

C   It permits gene exchange between homologous chromosomes.

D   It results in the independent assortment of chromosomes.

10. The transmission of a gene for deafness is shown in the family tree below.

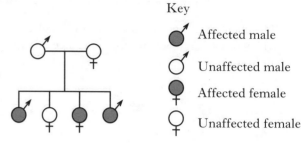

This condition is controlled by an allele which is

A   dominant and sex-linked

B   recessive and sex-linked

C   dominant and not sex-linked

D   recessive and not sex-linked.

11. The examination of a karyotype would **not** detect

A   phenylketonuria

B   Down's syndrome

C   the sex of the fetus

D   evidence of non-disjunction.

12. A woman with blood group AB has a child to a man with blood group O. What are the possible phenotypes of the child?

A A or B

B AB only

C AB or O

D AB, A or B

13. Cystic fibrosis is an inherited condition caused by a recessive allele. The diagram below is a family tree showing affected individuals.

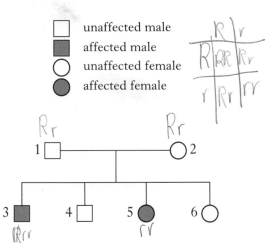

Which two individuals in this family tree must be heterozygous for the cystic fibrosis gene?

A   3 and 5

B   4 and 6

C   1 and 2

D   2 and 6

14. The diagram below shows the influence of the pituitary gland on testosterone production.

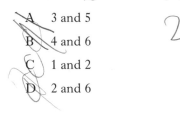

What is hormone X?

A   Luteinising hormone

B   Follicle stimulating hormone

C   Oestrogen

D   Progesterone

15. From which structure in the female reproductive system does a corpus luteum develop?

A   Endometrium

B   Graafian follicle

C   Fertilised ovum

D   Unfertilised ovum

16. The table below contains information about four semen samples.

	Semen sample			
	A	B	C	D
Number of sperm in sample (millions/cm^3)	40	30	20	60
Active sperm (percent)	50	60	75	40
Abnormal sperm (percent)	30	65	10	70

Which semen sample has the highest number of active sperm per cm^3?

17. Which of the following describes correctly the exchange of materials between maternal and fetal circulations?

	Glucose	Antibodies
A	into fetus by active transport	into fetus by active transport
B	into fetus by active transport	into fetus by pinocytosis
C	into fetus by pinocytosis	into fetus by active transport
D	into fetus by diffusion	into mother by pinocytosis

18. The diffusion pathway of carbon dioxide within body tissues is

A   plasma → tissue fluid → cell cytoplasm

B   lymph → tissue fluid → cell cytoplasm

C   cell cytoplasm → tissue fluid → plasma

D   tissue fluid → lymph → plasma.

[Turn over

19. The graph below shows changes in arterial blood pressure.

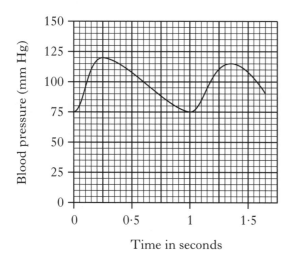

Time in seconds

The shape of the graph is due to

A   the action of the heart muscle

B   the action of the diaphragm

C   the closing of the valves in the veins

D   muscular contraction of the arteries.

20. An ECG trace is shown below.

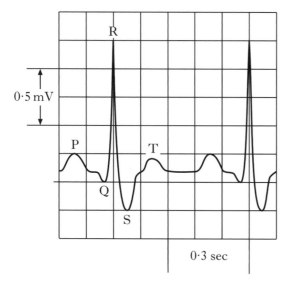

What is the person's heart rate?

A   100 beats per minute

B   120 beats per minute

C   150 beats per minute

D   200 beats per minute

21. Which of the following statements refers correctly to the cardiac cycle?

A   During systole the atria contract followed by the ventricles.

B   During systole the ventricles contract followed by the atria.

C   During diastole the atria contract followed by the ventricles.

D   During diastole the ventricles contract followed by the atria.

22. Which line in the table below correctly describes the conditions under which the affinity of haemoglobin for oxygen is highest?

	Oxygen tension	Temperature (°C)
A	high	40
B	high	37
C	low	37
D	low	40

23. Which of the following is triggered by the hypothalamus in response to an increase in the temperature of the body?

A   Contraction of the hair erector muscles and vasodilation of the skin arterioles

B   Contraction of the hair erector muscles and vasoconstriction of the skin arterioles

C   Relaxation of the hair erector muscles and vasodilation of the skin arterioles

D   Relaxation of the hair erector muscles and vasoconstriction of the skin arterioles

24. The graph below shows the rate of sweating of an individual in different environmental conditions.

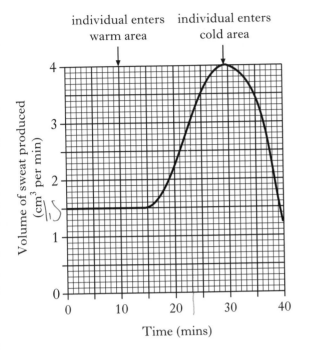

How long after entering the warm area did it take for the volume of sweat production to increase by 100%?

A   8 minutes

B   13 minutes

C   20 minutes

D   23 minutes

25. The diagram below shows the main parts of the brain as seen in vertical section.

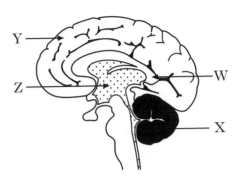

Which line in the table below correctly identifies the functions of two areas of the brain?

	Communication between hemispheres	Reasoning
A	W	X
B	X	Y
C	W	Y
D	Z	W

[Turn over

26. The diagram below shows a test on a man who had a damaged corpus callosum. This meant that he could no longer transfer information between his right and left cerebral hemispheres.

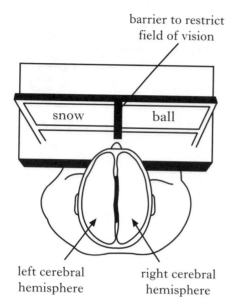

barrier to restrict field of vision

snow   ball

left cerebral hemisphere   right cerebral hemisphere

Some of the functions of each hemisphere are described in the table below.

Left cerebral hemisphere	Right cerebral hemisphere
processes information from right eye	processes information from left eye
controls language production	controls spatial task co-ordination

The man was asked to look straight ahead and then the words "snow" and "ball" were flashed briefly on the screen as shown.

What would the man say that he had just seen?

A Ball

B Snow

C Snowball

D Nothing

27. Which of the following statements about diverging neural pathways is correct?

A They accelerate the transmission of sensory impulses.

B They suppress the transmission of sensory impulses.

C They decrease the degree of fine motor control.

D They increase the degree of fine motor control.

28. Which of the following describes the change in an individual's behaviour where the presence of others causes the individual to show less restraint and become more impulsive?

A Social facilitation

B Shaping

C Generalisation

D Deindividuation

29. Which of the following identifies correctly a process in the nitrogen cycle?

A Nitrifying bacteria trap atmospheric nitrogen.

B Nitrifying bacteria convert ammonium compounds to nitrates.

C Nitrogen-fixing bacteria convert nitrates to atmospheric nitrogen.

D Denitrifying bacteria convert ammonia to nitrates.

30. The diagrams below contain information about the population of Britain.

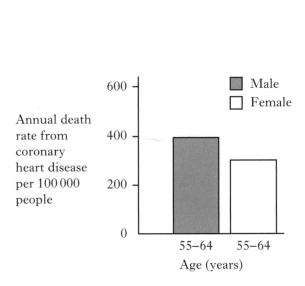

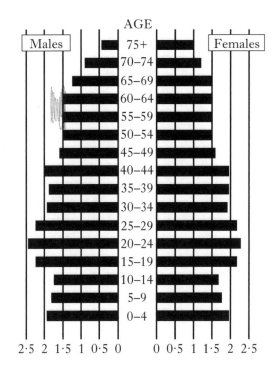

Population size (millions)

How many British men between 55 and 64 years of age die from coronary heart disease annually?

A   400

B   6000

C   12 000

D   24 000

**Candidates are reminded that the answer sheet MUST be returned
INSIDE the front cover of this answer booklet.**

[Turn over for Section B on *Page eleven*

[BLANK PAGE]

Marks

SECTION B

All questions in this section should be attempted.

All answers must be written clearly and legibly in ink.

1.   The diagram below represents stages in the production of human sperm.

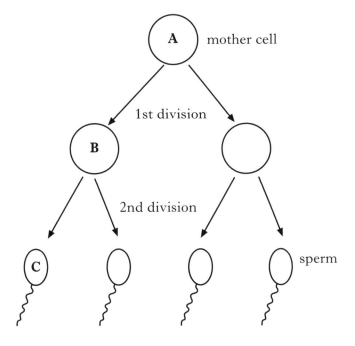

A mother cell

1st division

B

2nd division

C sperm

(a)   Name the type of cell division that produces sex cells.

Meiosis

1

(b)   State the number of chromosomes which would be present in the cells labelled A, B and C.

A: _____46_____   B: _____46_____   C: _____23_____

1

(c)   Compare the appearance of the chromosomes in cell B and cell C.

B would have the full compliment whereas C would be exactly half (with an X or Y chromosome depending on gender)

1

(d)   Name the **two** processes which increase variation during the 1st division of the sperm mother cell.

1 _____

2 _____

1

(e)   State the location of sperm production in the testes.

Seminiferous tubules

1

DO N
WRIT
TH
MAR(

Marks

2. The diagram below shows some of the reactions which occur during aerobic respiration.

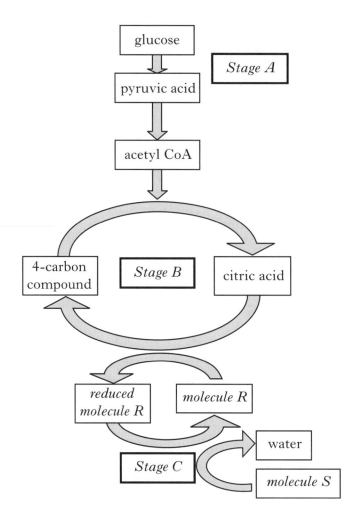

(a) Complete the table by naming stages A, B and C and indicating their **exact** location within the cell.

Stage	Name	Location
A	Glycolysis	Cytoplasm
B	Citric acid cycle	Matrix of mitochondria
C	O transport chain	Membrane of mitochondria

3

(b) A glucose molecule contains 6 carbon atoms.

How many carbon atoms are found in the following molecules?

Pyruvic acid ___2___

Citric acid ___4___

1

DO NOT WRITE IN THIS MARGIN

Marks

2. (continued)

(*c*) Complete the following sentences by naming molecules R and S and describing their function with respect to stage C.

R is NADH ~~and~~ and its function is to bring H^+ and high energy e^- to the e^- transport chain.

S is Oxygen and its function is the final H acceptor. **2**

(*d*) Under normal circumstances carbohydrate is the main respiratory substrate.

In each of the following extreme situations, state the alternative respiratory substrate and explain why the body has to use it.

Situation	*Respiratory substrate*	*Explanation*
Prolonged starvation	Fat	No glucose/sugars are made available
Towards the end of a marathon race	Creatine phosphate	ATP reserves are used up

2

[Turn over

Marks

3. The diagram below shows blood from a person who has been infected by bacteria. These bacteria have triggered an immune response involving proteins P and Q.

The diagram is not drawn to scale.

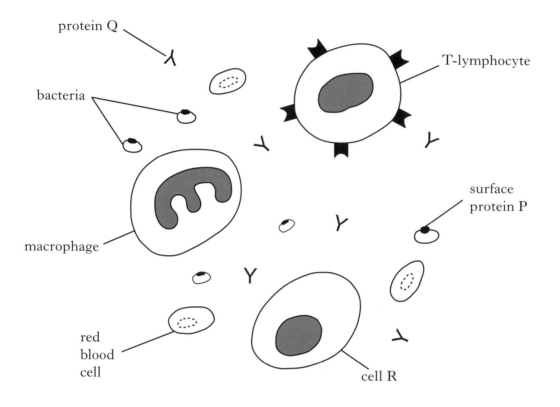

(a) (i) Identify proteins P and Q.

P _____   Q _____   **1**

(ii) Cell R produced protein Q.

Name this type of cell.

_____   **1**

(iii) Describe the role of the following cells in combating infection.

(A) T-lymphocyte _____

_____   **1**

(B) Macrophage _____

_____   **1**

DO NOT WRITE IN THIS MARGIN

Marks

3. (continued)

(*b*) Complete the following sentences by underlining one option from each pair of options shown in **bold**.

(i) Immunity gained after contracting a bacterial infection is an example of **active** / **passive** immunity that is **naturally** / **artificially** acquired. **1**

(ii) Immunity gained from the injection of a tetanus vaccine is an example of **active** / **passive** immunity that is **naturally** / **artificially** acquired. **1**

(*c*) What happens during an autoimmune response?

____

____ **1**

[Turn over

Marks

4. Lactose is the main sugar found in milk.

    Lactose is broken down by lactase, an enzyme which is made by cells lining the small intestine. The glucose and galactose molecules produced are then absorbed into the bloodstream.

    $$\text{lactose} \xrightarrow{\text{lactase}} \text{glucose} + \text{galactose}$$

    A student carried out an investigation to compare the lactose content of human milk and cow milk.

    He set up a test tube containing human milk and lactase solution. Every 30 seconds samples were taken and the glucose concentration measured. Then he repeated the procedure with cow milk.

    His experimental setup is shown in Figure 1.

    His results are shown in the table below.

Time (min)	Concentration of glucose (%)	
	Human milk	Cow milk
0	0	0
0·5	0·28	0·28
1·0	0·54	0·46
1·5	0·80	0·54
2·0	1·04	0·58
2·5	1·10	0·58
3·0	1·10	0·58

Figure 1

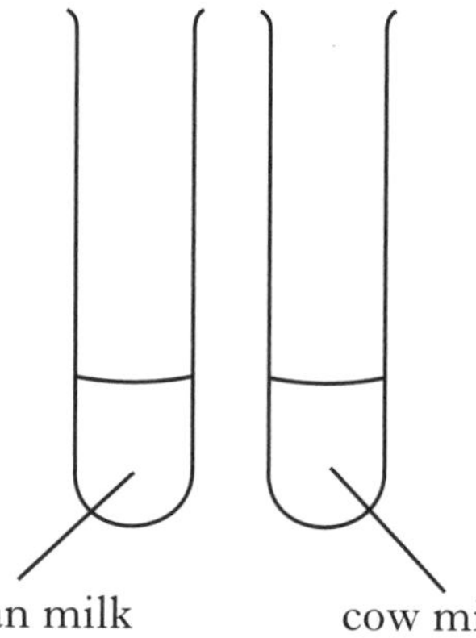

human milk and lactase   cow milk and lactase

(a) Lactose is a disaccharide sugar.

    Explain how the information above supports this statement.

    _____

    _____   1

(b) One variable that must be kept constant in this investigation is pH.

    List **two** other variables which would have to be kept constant.

    1 _____

    2 _____   1

DO NOT
WRITE IN
THIS
MARGIN

Marks

4. **(continued)**

(*c*) Construct a line graph to show all the data in the table.

(Additional graph paper, if required, can be found on *Page thirty-six.*)

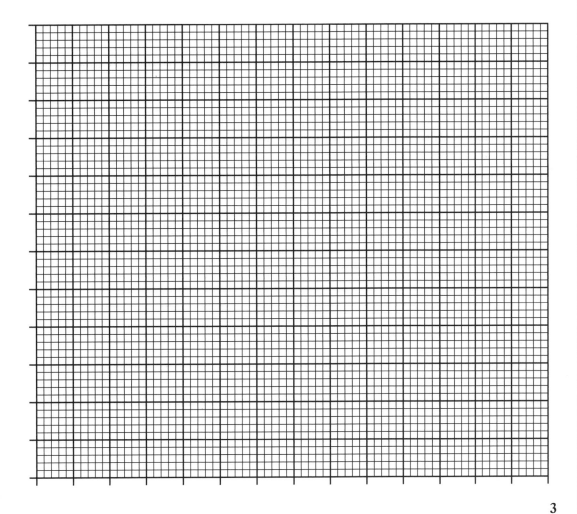

3

(*d*) What conclusion can be drawn from this investigation?

_____

_____ 1

(*e*) Suggest a reason why the rate of glucose production is not constant throughout the investigation.

_____

_____ 1

(*f*) How could the student improve the reliability of his results?

_____

_____ 1

Marks

4. (continued)

(*g*) Some people who have problems digesting lactose are said to be lactose intolerant.

They cannot produce the enzyme lactase.

(i) What general phrase describes an inherited disorder in which the absence of an enzyme prevents a chemical reaction from happening?

_____   1

(ii) A test can be carried out for lactose intolerance.

The individual being tested does not eat for twelve hours and then drinks a liquid that contains lactose. The individual rests for the next two hours during which their blood glucose level is measured at regular intervals.

What results would be expected if the individual is lactose intolerant?

_____

_____   1

Marks

5. The diagram below shows a section of a woman's breast shortly after she has given birth.

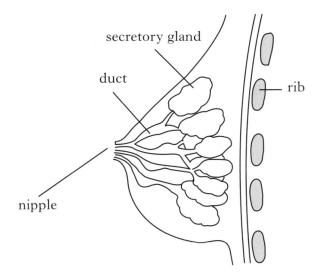

(a) (i) Name the hormone that stimulates the secretory glands to start producing milk.

_____

1

(ii) The cells lining the secretory glands are particularly rich in ribosomes. Suggest a reason for this.

_____

_____

1

(b) Fluid is not usually released from the breast until the baby suckles.

(i) What name is given to the first fluid that the baby receives from the breast?

_____

1

(ii) Describe **one** way in which this first fluid differs from the breast milk produced a few days later.

_____

_____

1

(iii) Suckling and crying are examples of non-verbal communication used by a baby. Why is non-verbal communication important to **both** the mother and baby?

_____

_____

1

Marks

6. The flow diagram below summarises what happens in the body after a meal of fish and chips.

```
┌─────────────────────────────────────────┐
│   Digestion of fish and chips in the     │
│       stomach and small intestine        │
└─────────────────────────────────────────┘
                    │
                    ▼
┌─────────────────────────────────────────┐
│  Absorption of the products of digestion │
│  through the walls of the small intestine│
└─────────────────────────────────────────┘
                    │
                    ▼
┌─────────────────────────────────────────┐
│      Metabolism of some absorbed         │
│          substances by the liver         │
└─────────────────────────────────────────┘
                    │
                    ▼
┌─────────────────────────────────────────┐
│   Transport of some products of metabolism│
│     around the body in the bloodstream    │
└─────────────────────────────────────────┘
```

(a) Explain how bile salts aid the digestion of the fish and chips.

_____

_____   1

(b) The products of fat digestion are fatty acids and glycerol.

Describe the route taken by these products as they move from the small intestine to the bloodstream.

_____

_____

_____

_____   2

DO NOT WRITE IN THIS MARGIN

Marks

6. (continued)

(*c*) During the absorption and metabolism of this meal, samples of blood from the hepatic portal vein and the hepatic vein were tested for glucose and urea.

Complete each row of the table below, using the words **Higher** and **Lower**, to compare the concentration of each substance in the two blood vessels.

	Blood vessel	
Substance	Hepatic portal vein	Hepatic vein
Glucose		
Urea		

2

(*d*) State **one** feature of veins which helps to maintain blood flow.

____

____ 1

(*e*) Drugs and alcohol pass into the bloodstream through the digestive system.

The liver converts these harmful substances into harmless products.

What term describes this action of the liver?

________________________ 1

[Turn over

7. A long distance runner took part in some laboratory tests using a treadmill.

She was asked to use the treadmill at a setting of 4 km/h for three minutes during which her pulse rate was monitored. At the end of this time a blood sample was taken which was tested for lactic acid concentration. The procedure was then repeated a number of times at faster speeds.

The results of the tests are shown in the graph below.

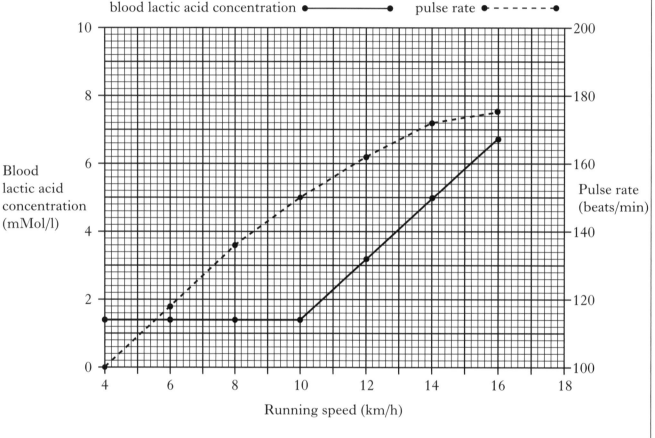

blood lactic acid concentration ●————● 　 pulse rate ●- - - - - -●

(Blood lactic acid concentration (mMol/l) vs Running speed (km/h); Pulse rate (beats/min))

(a) (i)   What was the runner's pulse rate when she was running at 6 km/h?

_____   **1**

(ii) State the concentration of lactic acid in the runner's blood when her pulse rate was 172 beats/min.

_____ mMol/l   **1**

(iii) Predict what the runner's blood lactic acid concentration would be if she ran at 18 km/h for three minutes.

Blood lactic acid concentration _____ mMol/l   **1**

DO NOT WRITE IN THIS MARGIN

Marks

7. (continued)

(*b*) A build-up of lactic acid in muscles leads to fatigue.

(i) Explain why lactic acid builds up in the muscles as running speeds increase.

____

____

____

____ **2**

(ii) Distance runners often monitor their pulse rate while they are training.

Suggest how this runner could use a pulse rate monitor and the information from the graph to allow her to run for long periods of time without developing muscle fatigue.

____

____

____

____ **2**

[Turn over

DO N
WRIT
TH
MAR(

Marks

8. Two men (P and R) were being tested for *diabetes mellitus*, a condition which results in failure to control blood glucose concentration.

   After fasting overnight, they were given a large glucose drink. Their blood glucose concentration was measured immediately (0 hours) and then every hour for five hours.

   The results of the tests are shown in the table below.

	Time after drinking glucose (hours)					
	0	*1*	*2*	*3*	*4*	*5*
Blood glucose concentration of P (mg/100 ml)	145	210	190	180	170	160
Blood glucose concentration of R (mg/100 ml)	90	125	90	85	90	90

   (a) It was concluded that P had diabetes and R did not.

   (i) State **two** ways in which the test results indicate that P has diabetes.

   1 _____

   2 _____   1

   (ii) Name the hormone responsible for the change in the blood glucose concentration of R

   (A) between 1 and 2 hours   _____

   (B) between 3 and 4 hours.   _____   1

   (b) *Diabetes insipidus* can be caused by a lack of ADH in the body.

   (i) Which organ of the body releases ADH?

   _____   1

   (ii) State an effect that failure to produce ADH would have on the body.

   _____

   _____   1

Marks

9. The diagram below shows a synapse between two nerve cells in the brain and a magnified view of a receptor called NMDA.

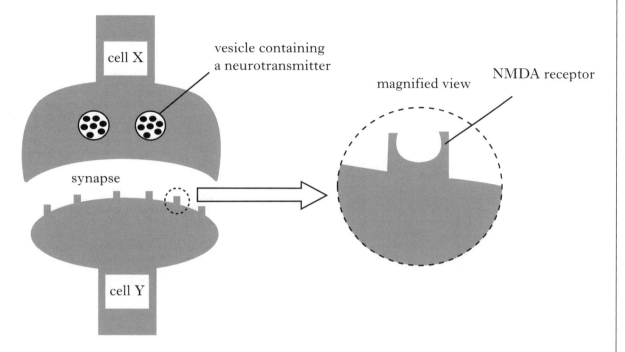

(a) (i) Describe how the neurotransmitter in the vesicle reaches cell Y.

_____

_____

_____   2

(ii) The diagram above shows a single neural pathway.

Explain how a converging neural pathway would be more likely to generate an impulse in nerve cell Y.

_____

_____

_____   2

(b) Many factors can lead to memory loss.

(i) One of these factors is a reduction in the number of NMDA receptors.

Which part of the brain contains nerve cells rich in NMDA receptors?

_____   1

(ii) Another factor is the decreased production of acetylcholine.

Name the condition which results from the loss of acetylcholine-producing cells in the brain.

_____   1

DO N
WRITE
THI
MARG

Marks

10. A study was carried out to compare the influence of genetics with that of the environment on the development of two behavioural conditions, A and B.

Several hundred pairs of children, from the same families, took part in the study. Some pairs were monozygotic twins, some pairs were dizygotic twins and some pairs were adopted and unrelated.

In each pair, one of the children had one of the behavioural conditions and investigators observed whether or not the other child shared the condition.

Results of the study are shown in the bar graph below.

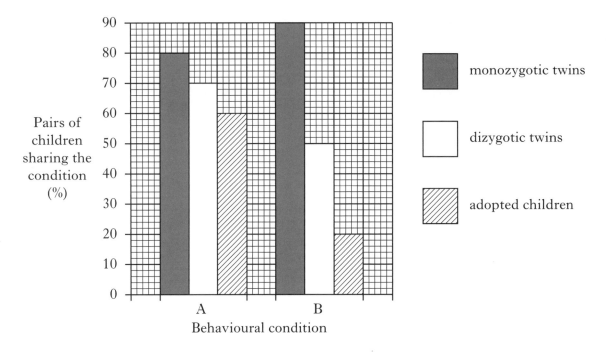

(a) Explain why it was important that monozygotic twins were chosen for this study.

_____

_____

_____   2

(b) Use the graph to explain whether conditions A and B are more likely to be caused by genetic or environmental factors.

(i) Likely cause of condition A _____

Explanation _____

_____   1

(ii) Likely cause of condition B _____

Explanation _____

_____   1

Marks

11. The bar graph shows population changes in Scotland for different age groups between 1991 and 2000.

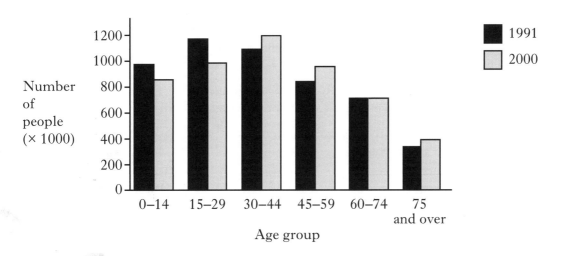

(a) Suggest a reason for the population change in those aged 75 and over.

_____

_____ 1

(b) Describe **two** ways in which the data for the year 2000 would be different if it were taken from a developing country with a similar population size to Scotland.

1 _____

_____

2 _____

_____ 1

(c) Describe **two** ways in which the information in the graph could be used by authorities to plan for the future.

1 _____

_____

2 _____

_____ 1

[Turn over

Marks

12. An investigation was carried out into the influence of adults on the behaviour of young children.

    Some groups of children watched a recording of either a man or a woman being physically and verbally aggressive to a large plastic clown.

    Other groups of children watched either a man or a woman behaving in a non-aggressive manner towards the clown.

    Each child was then placed in a room on their own with the clown. The number of aggressive acts they committed over a five minute period was counted.

    The figures in the table below show the average number of aggressive acts that the children committed while in the room.

Gender of children	*Average number of aggressive acts committed by the children*			
	Aggressive man observed	*Aggressive woman observed*	*Non-aggressive man observed*	*Non-aggressive woman observed*
Boys	18·7	7·9	1·0	0·6
Girls	4·4	9·2	0·2	0·8

(a) (i) Which adult/child combination resulted in the least aggression?

    _____ 　1

    (ii) Calculate the percentage increase in aggressive acts committed by boys when they observe an aggressive man rather than a non-aggressive man.

    Space for calculation

    _____ %　1

    (iii) State a conclusion that can be drawn from these results regarding the gender of the aggressive adult.

    _____

    _____ 　1

(b) The children are observing and then repeating the acts of adults. What form of learning are they using?

    _____　1

(c) Suggest a control that could have also been used in this investigation.

    _____

    _____ 　1

13. The graph below shows the application rates of nitrogen and phosphorus to crops in an area of Scotland between 1986 and 2006.

Marks

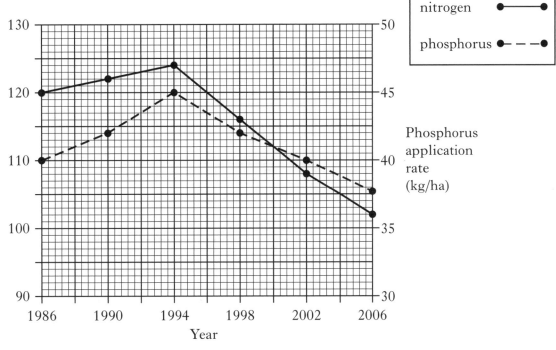

(*a*) Describe **one** similarity and **one** difference in the data for nitrogen and phosphorus application rate between 1986 and 2006.

Similarity _____

_____

Difference _____

_____   **2**

(*b*) Express, as a simple whole number ratio, the application rate of nitrogen compared to phosphorus in 1986.

Space for calculation

_____ : _____   **1**
nitrogen   phosphorus

(*c*) In recent years, there has been a decrease in the use of nitrogen and phosphorus on farms in Scotland.

(i) Suggest **one** way in which this decrease might benefit the environment.

_____

_____   **1**

(ii) Suggest **one** way in which this decrease might disadvantage farmers.

_____

_____   **1**

Marks

14. Glaciers are large masses of ice on mountains and in cold regions of the world. The graph below shows the average change in glacier thickness around the world between 1955 and 2005.

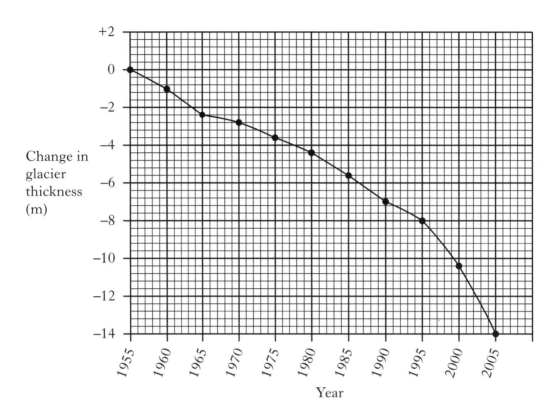

(*a*) (i) Calculate the average yearly decrease in glacier thickness between 1955 and 2005.

Space for calculation

_____ m/year   **1**

(ii) One consequence of this decrease in glacier thickness is rising sea levels. Describe **one** effect of rising sea levels and subsequent flooding on coastal communities around the world.

_____

_____   **1**

Marks

14. (continued)

(b) Many people believe that the change in glacier thickness is caused by global warming.

   (i) Name **two** gases that contribute to global warming.

     1 _____ 2 _____   **1**

   (ii) Give **two** reasons why one of these gases is increasing in the atmosphere.

     Gas _____

     Reason 1 _____

     _____

     Reason 2 _____

     _____   **1**

[Turn over for Section C on *Page thirty-two*

DO N
WRITI
THI
MARC

Marks

SECTION C

Both questions in this section should be attempted.

Note that each question contains a choice.

Questions 1 and 2 should be attempted on the blank pages which follow.

Supplementary sheets, if required, may be obtained from the Invigilator.

Labelled diagrams may be used where appropriate.

1. Answer **either** A **or** B.

    A. Discuss memory under the following headings:

        (i) short-term memory;   **5**

        (ii) the transfer of information between short and long-term memory.   **5**

        (10)

    OR

    B. Discuss how man has attempted to increase food supply under the following headings:

        (i) chemical use;   **4**

        (ii) genetic improvement;   **3**

        (iii) land use.   **3**

        (10)

In question 2, ONE mark is available for coherence and ONE mark is available for relevance.

2. Answer **either** A **or** B.

    A. Discuss the biological basis of contraception.   **(10)**

    OR

    B. Discuss the conducting system of the heart and how it is controlled.   **(10)**

[END OF QUESTION PAPER]

HIGHER

2011

[BLANK PAGE]

FOR OFFICIAL USE

Total for
Sections B & C

X009/301

| NATIONAL QUALIFICATIONS 2011 | WEDNESDAY, 1 JUNE 1.00 PM – 3.30 PM | HUMAN BIOLOGY HIGHER |

Fill in these boxes and read what is printed below.

Full name of centre

Town

Forename(s)

Surname

Date of birth

Day   Month   Year   Scottish candidate number

Number of seat

SECTION A—Questions 1–30

Instructions for completion of Section A are given on page two.

For this section of the examination you must use an **HB pencil**.

SECTIONS B AND C

1 (a) All questions should be attempted.

(b) It should be noted that in **Section C** questions 1 and 2 each contain a choice.

2 The questions may be answered in any order but all answers are to be written in the spaces provided in this answer book, **and must be written clearly and legibly in ink**.

3 Additional space for answers will be found at the end of the book. If further space is required, supplementary sheets may be obtained from the Invigilator and should be inserted inside the **front** cover of this book.

4 The numbers of questions must be clearly inserted with any answers written in the additional space.

5 Rough work, if any should be necessary, should be written in this book and then scored through when the fair copy has been written. If further space is required a supplementary sheet for rough work may be obtained from the Invigilator.

6 Before leaving the examination room you must give this book to the Invigilator. If you do not, you may lose all the marks for this paper.

Read carefully

1   Check that the answer sheet provided is for **Human Biology Higher (Section A)**.

2   For this section of the examination you must use an **HB pencil**, and where necessary, an eraser.

3   Check that the answer sheet you have been given has **your name**, **date of birth**, **SCN** (Scottish Candidate Number) and **Centre Name** printed on it.

Do not change any of these details.

4   If any of this information is wrong, tell the Invigilator immediately.

5   If this information is correct, **print** your name and seat number in the boxes provided.

6   The answer to each question is **either** A, B, C or D. Decide what your answer is, then, using your pencil, put a horizontal line in the space provided (see sample question below).

7   There is **only one correct** answer to each question.

8   Any rough working should be done on the question paper or the rough working sheet, **not** on your answer sheet.

9   At the end of the examination, put the **answer sheet for Section A inside the front cover of this answer book**.

Sample Question

The digestive enzyme pepsin is most active in the

A   stomach

B   mouth

C   duodenum

D   pancreas.

The correct answer is **A**—stomach. The answer **A** has been clearly marked in **pencil** with a horizontal line (see below).

Changing an answer

If you decide to change your answer, carefully erase your first answer and, using your pencil, fill in the answer you want. The answer below has been changed to **D**.

A   B   C   D

SECTION A

All questions in this section should be attempted.

Answers should be given on the separate answer sheet provided.

1. A DNA molecule consists of 4000 nucleotides of which 20% contain the base adenine.

   How many of the nucleotides in this DNA molecule will contain guanine?

   A   800

   B   1000

   C   1200

   D   1600

2. The function of tRNA in cell metabolism is to

   A   transport amino acids to be used in synthesis

   B   carry codons to the ribosomes

   C   synthesise proteins

   D   transcribe the DNA code.

3. The Golgi apparatus is involved in the packaging of

   A   ribosomes

   B   monosaccharides

   C   RNA

   D   enzymes.

4. Which of the following cells secrete antibodies?

   A   B-lymphocytes

   B   T-lymphocytes

   C   Red blood cells

   D   Macrophages

5. The diagram below summarises different types of immunity.

   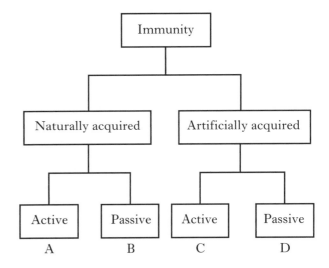

   Which type of immunity would arise from breast feeding?

6. Haemophilia is a sex-linked recessive condition. A woman, who does not have this condition, has a haemophiliac son. The boy's father is also a haemophiliac.

   What are the genotypes of the parents?

	Father	Mother
A	X^HY	X^HX^h
B	X^hY	X^hX^h
C	X^hY	X^HX^H
D	X^hY	X^HX^h

[Turn over

7. The table below shows the results of chemical tests on five carbohydrates.

Carbohydrate	Chemical test			
	Iodine solution	Benedict's solution	Barfoed's reagent	Clinistix strip
starch	turns blue-black	stays blue	stays blue	stays pink
sucrose	stays brown	stays blue	stays blue	stays pink
lactose	stays brown	turns orange	stays blue	stays pink
fructose	stays brown	turns orange	turns orange	stays pink
glucose	stays brown	turns orange	turns orange	turns purple

What is the minimum number of tests that would need to be carried out to identify an unknown carbohydrate as lactose?

A   one

B   two

C   three

D   four

8. Huntington's Disease is an inherited condition in humans caused by a dominant allele which is not sex-linked.

A woman's father is heterozygous for the condition and her mother is unaffected.

What is the chance of the woman having the condition?

A   1 in 1

B   1 in 2

C   1 in 3

D   1 in 4

9. The cell shown below is magnified six hundred times. What is the actual size of the cell?

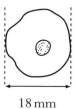

18 mm

A   1080 μm

B   108 μm

C   30 μm

D   3 μm

10. The diagram shows the chromosome complement of cells during the development of abnormal human sperm.

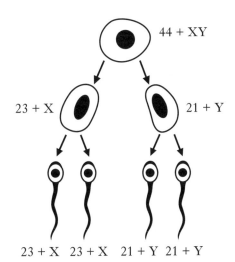

A sperm with chromosome complement 23+X fertilises a normal haploid egg. What is the chromosome number and sex of the resulting zygote?

	Chromosome number	Sex of zygote
A	24	female
B	46	female
C	46	male
D	47	female

11. In fertility clinics, samples of semen are collected for testing.

The table below shows the analysis of semen samples taken from five men.

Semen sample	1	2	3	4	5
Number of sperm in sample (millions/cm³)	40	19	25	45	90
Active sperm (percent)	65	60	75	10	70
Abnormal sperm (percent)	30	20	90	30	10

A man is fertile if his semen contains at least 20 million sperm cells/cm^3 and at least 60% of the sperm cells are active and at least 60% of the sperm cells are normal.

The semen samples that were taken from infertile men are

A   samples 3 and 4 only

B   samples 2 and 4 only

C   samples 2, 3 and 4 only

D   samples 1, 2, 4 and 5 only.

12. The graphs below show the hormones involved in the menstrual cycle.

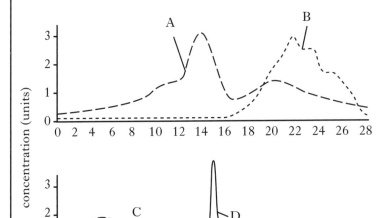

Which line represents oestrogen?

13. The vein in the umbilical cord carries

   A   oxygenated fetal blood

   B   deoxygenated fetal blood

   C   oxygenated maternal blood

   D   deoxygenated maternal blood.

14. A child born to parents with different Rhesus factors can be at risk because

   A   anti-D antibodies from the Rh− mother destroy the baby's red blood cells

   B   anti-D antibodies from the Rh+ mother destroy the baby's red blood cells

   C   anti-D antigens from the Rh− mother destroy the baby's red blood cells

   D   anti-D antigens from the Rh+ mother destroy the baby's red blood cells.

15. The diagram below shows the blood supply to cells lining an air sac in the lungs.

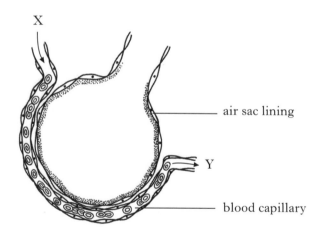

Which line of the table shows correctly the change in concentration of glucose and oxygen as the blood flows from X to Y?

	Glucose	Oxygen
A	increase	increase
B	increase	decrease
C	decrease	increase
D	decrease	decrease

16. The diagram below shows the liver and its associated blood vessels.

   The arrows show the direction of blood flow.

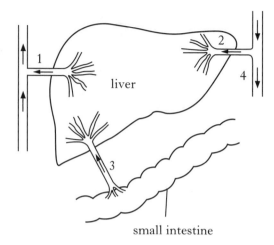

Which of the blood vessels are veins?

   A   1 and 2

   B   1 and 3

   C   2 and 3

   D   2 and 4

17. Which of the following is **not** a function of the lymphatic system?

   A   Production of tissue fluid

   B   Absorption of products from fat digestion

   C   Removal of bacteria

   D   Production of lymphocytes

18. Which of the following statements about red blood cells is true?

   A   They are manufactured in the liver.

   B   They have a lifespan of 240 days.

   C   Vitamin B_{12} is required for their production.

   D   They are broken down in the kidney.

19. The graph below shows how female bone density changes with age.

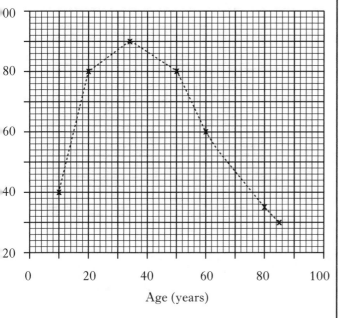

When a female's bone density falls to 60% of its maximum, there is an increased chance of bone breakage.

This occurs at

A   60 years

B   64 years

C   76 years

D   84 years.

20. Mature red blood cells have no nucleus and no mitochondria.

Which of the following processes can be carried out by a mature red blood cell?

A   Aerobic respiration

B   Protein synthesis

C   Anaerobic respiration

D   Cell division

21. Which of the following blood vessels is likely to contain blood with the lowest concentration of urea?

A   Hepatic artery

B   Hepatic vein

C   Renal artery

D   Renal vein

22. Which of the following correctly identifies the locations of the centres that monitor blood water concentration and temperature in humans?

	Blood water concentration	Temperature
A	Hypothalamus	Hypothalamus
B	Hypothalamus	Pituitary gland
C	Pituitary gland	Hypothalamus
D	Pituitary gland	Pituitary gland

23. Infants are more likely to suffer from hypothermia because they have

A   a low surface area to volume ratio

B   a high surface area to volume ratio

C   a low metabolic rate

D   a high metabolic rate.

24. When the body temperature becomes too high, which of the following sets of changes can occur in the skin?

A   Vasoconstriction and contraction of erector muscles

B   Vasodilation and contraction of erector muscles

C   Vasoconstriction and relaxation of erector muscles

D   Vasodilation and relaxation of erector muscles

25. The diagram below shows reactions involved in deamination.

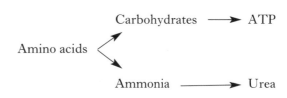

The reactions shown take place in the

A   small intestine

B   kidney

C   gall bladder

D   liver.

26. Which of the following statements is correct?

A The somatic nervous system controls mainly involuntary actions using sensory nerves.

B The somatic nervous system controls mainly voluntary actions using sympathetic nerves.

C The autonomic nervous system controls some involuntary actions using parasympathetic nerves.

D The autonomic nervous system controls some voluntary actions using motor nerves.

27. A young person does not smoke because she has seen an advertising campaign showing pictures of famous sports stars who do not smoke.

This is an example of a behaviour called

A identification

B discrimination

C generalisation

D deindividuation.

28. Which of the following best describes shaping behaviour?

The reward of behaviour which

A improves performance in competitive situations

B approximates to the desired behaviour

C results in the learning of motor skills

D results in deindividuation taking place.

29. The graph below shows the birth rate and death rate of a population.

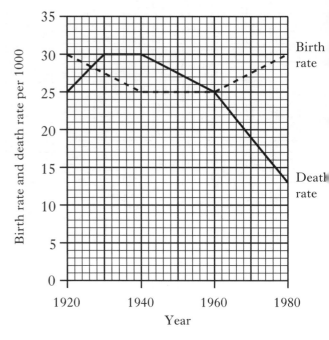

The year of greatest increase in population was

A 1920

B 1940

C 1960

D 1980.

30. When fertilisers enter a loch, the population of bacteria often increases dramatically.

Which line in the table below describes correctly the cause of the increase in the bacterial population and the result of the increase in the bacterial population?

	Cause of the increase in population of bacteria	Result of the increase in population of bacteria
A	death of plants	increase in nitrates
B	decrease in oxygen levels	increase in organic matter
C	increase in nitrates	algal blooms
D	increase in organic matter	decrease in oxygen levels

Candidates are reminded that the answer sheet MUST be returned INSIDE the front cover of this answer booklet.

[Turn over for Section B on *Page ten*

DO N
WRIT
TH
MAR

Marks

SECTION B

All questions in this section should be attempted.

All answers must be written clearly and legibly in ink.

1. (a) The diagram shows part of an mRNA molecule being formed on a strand of DNA.

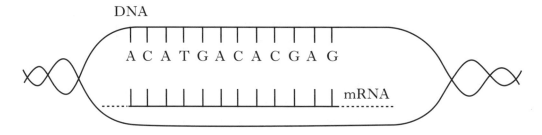

   (i) In which part of the cell is mRNA formed?

   _____   1

   (ii) Complete the mRNA molecule by filling in the correct base sequence **on the diagram.**   1

   (iii) How many amino acids are coded for by this section of mRNA?

   _____   1

   (b) Some diseases are caused when cells in the body produce a harmful protein. Recent research has led to the development of antisense drugs to treat such diseases. These drugs carry a short strand of RNA nucleotides designed to attach to a small part of the mRNA molecule that codes for the harmful protein.

   (i) Suggest how these drugs may prevent the production of a harmful protein.

   _____

   _____   1

   (ii) Antisense drugs can be used to treat autoimmune diseases.

   Describe what is meant by an autoimmune disease.

   _____

   _____   1

Marks

2. The diagram below shows a magnified section of the cell membrane of a red blood cell. The numbers show the relative concentrations of potassium ions that are maintained on either side of the membrane.

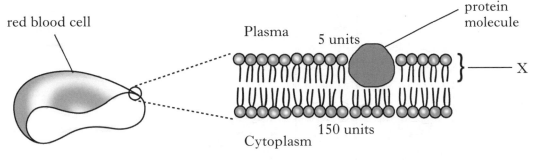

(a) Name molecule X.

_____   **1**

(b) State **one** possible function of the protein molecule shown in the diagram.

_____

_____   **1**

(c) Express, as a simple whole number ratio, the concentration of potassium ions inside and outside the cell.

Space for calculation

_____ : _____

inside   outside   **1**

(d) Use the information in the diagram to name the process by which potassium ions would leave the cell.

_____   **1**

(e) A sample of blood was treated with a chemical that inhibits respiration.

   (i) Describe how this treatment would change the relative concentrations of potassium ions on each side of the membrane.

   _____

   _____   **1**

   (ii) Explain why the relative concentrations would change.

   _____

   _____   **1**

DO N
WRIT
TH
MAR

Marks

3. The graph below shows the mass of DNA present as gamete mother cells develop into sperm cells during meoisis in the testes. P and Q represent cells at intermediate stages in this process.

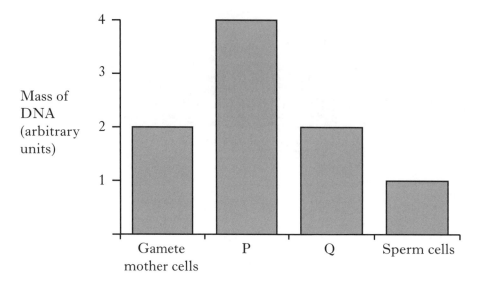

(a) Explain why the mass of DNA changes between

(i) the gamete mother cells and cell type P _____

_____ **1**

(ii) cell types P and Q. _____

_____ **1**

Marks

3. (continued)

(b) The diagram below shows a pair of chromosomes in a cell undergoing meiosis.

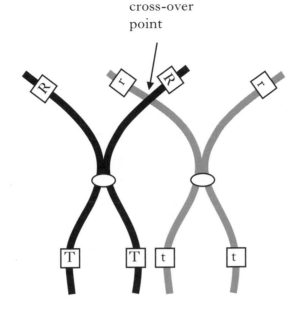

cross-over
point

Letters R and T represent dominant alleles of two different genes.

(i) What name is given to the point on the chromosomes where crossing over occurs?

_____

1

(ii) Assuming that crossing over does occur, give all the combinations of alleles that would be present in the resulting gametes.

_____

1

(iii) Crossing over leads to genetic variation.

Name **one** other way in which meiosis increases variation.

_____

1

(c) State the exact location of meiosis in the testes.

_____

1

[Turn over

Marks

4. The diagram below shows inheritance of the ABO blood group over three generations of a family. The letters represent the blood group of each individual.

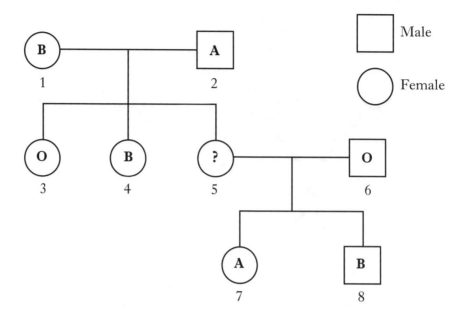

(a) The ABO blood group system is controlled by three alleles: *A*, *B* and *O*. Alleles *A* and *B* are co-dominant and both are completely dominant to allele *O*.

   (i) State the genotypes of the following:

   Individual 1 _____

   Individual 3 _____   1

   (ii) What is the blood group of individual 5? Give a reason for your answer.

   Blood group _____

   Reason_____

   _____

   _____   2

   (iii) How many of the individuals shown in the family tree have a genotype which is heterozygous?

   _____   1

(b) During an operation, individual 4 needed a blood transfusion.

   Identify all the individuals in the family tree who could safely donate blood to her.

   _____   1

Marks

5. The diagrams represent gamete production in an ovary and part of a testis.

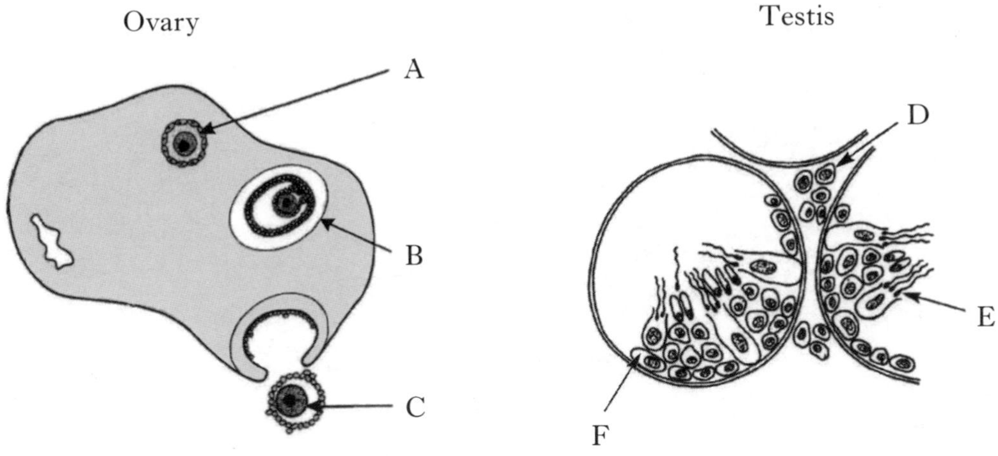

Ovary

Testis

(a) (i) Which letter represents a mature ovum?

_____

1

(ii) Identify **one** labelled part of each organ which is affected by FSH.

Letter	Name

2

(iii) Describe the effect of testosterone on the testes of an adult.

_____

_____

1

(b) Oxytocin is a hormone which is secreted during and after childbirth.

(i) State where oxytocin is produced in the body.

_____

1

(ii) Synthetic oxytocin can be used to induce labour.
Describe how it brings about birth.

_____

_____

1

[Turn over

Marks

6. The diagram shows a kidney nephron.

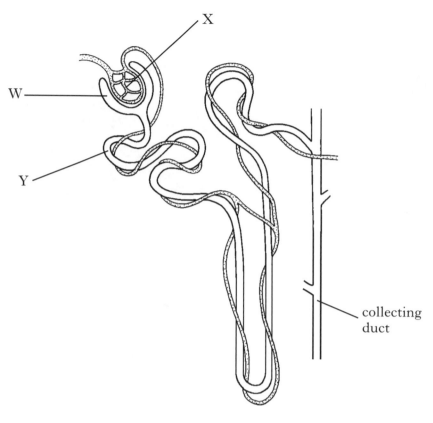

(a) (i) Name structure W.

_____   **1**

(ii) High blood pressure causes fluid to move from X to W.

Name this process and explain what causes the high blood pressure within X.

Process _____   **1**

Explanation _____

_____   **1**

(b) (i) Name structure Y.

_____   **1**

(ii) Describe the main process that occurs in structure Y.

_____

_____   **1**

Marks

6. **(continued)**

(c) The graph below shows how changes in the concentration of ADH in the blood affect the production rate and solute concentration of urine.

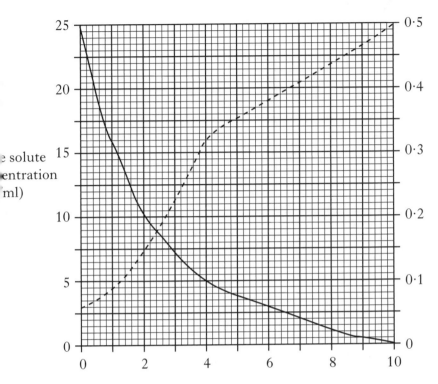

urine solute concentration (mg/ml)

urine production rate (l/hour)

concentration of ADH in blood (mg/l)

Legend:
—— urine production rate
- - - - urine solute concentration

(i) **Use the graph** to describe **two** effects of increasing the concentration of ADH in the blood.

1 _____

_____

2 _____

_____   **1**

(ii) What is the urine solute concentration when the ADH concentration in the blood is 6 mg/l?

_____   **1**

(iii) What is the urine production rate when the urine solute concentration is 4 mg/ml?

_____ litres/hour   **1**

(iv) If the ADH concentration in the blood remains constant at 4 mg/l, calculate the mass of solute excreted in the urine in one hour.

Space for calculation

_____ mg   **1**

DO N
WRIT
TH
MAR

Marks

7. (*a*) The diagram represents a section through the heart.

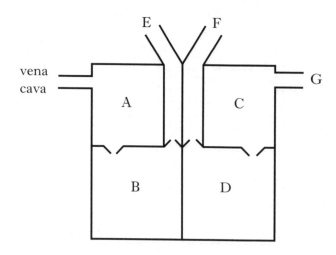

(i) Name blood vessels E and F.

Vessel E _____

Vessel F _____   1

(ii) State **two** differences between the composition of the blood in chambers B and D.

1 _____

2 _____   1

(iii) Place a cross (**X**) on the diagram to indicate the position of the sinoatrial node (SAN).   1

(iv) Describe the effect of the autonomic nervous system on the sinoatrial node (SAN).

_____

_____

_____

_____   2

(*b*) State the function of the coronary artery.

_____   1

DO NOT
WRITE IN
THIS
MARGIN

Marks

8. The table below contains information about diagnosed cases of diabetes in the four countries of the UK in 2008.

Country	Population (million)	Individuals diagnosed with diabetes (% of population)
England	51·3	3·9
Scotland	5·4	3·7
Wales	3·2	4·4
Northern Ireland	1·8	3·4
Total	61·7	

(a) Use the data in the table to calculate the number of individuals in the Scottish population who had diabetes in 2008.

Space for calculation

_____   1

(b) A student calculated the percentage of the UK population that had been diagnosed with diabetes by averaging the percentage values in the table. Suggest why this average is likely to misrepresent the true percentage of people in the UK who have been diagnosed with diabetes.

_____

_____   1

(c) It has been suggested that the number of people in the UK with diabetes will double by the year 2030.

Suggest **two** different ways in which the current UK government might use this information to plan for the future.

1 _____

_____

2 _____

_____   1

[**Turn over**

Marks

8. **(continued)**

(d) The graph below contains information about the number of people in Scotland who consulted their doctor about diabetes in 2008.

People consulting about diabetes (per 1000 people)

□ males

■ females

Age group (years)

(i) For people aged between 25 and 74 describe **one** trend shown by the graph which relates to

age _____

_____

gender _____

_____ **1**

(ii) In a Scottish city 2500 men between 45 and 54 years of age visited their doctor in 2008.

Use the graph to calculate how many of these men would be consulting their doctor about diabetes.

Space for calculation

_____ **1**

(iii) Calculate the percentage decrease in the number of men consulting their doctor between the 65-74 age group and the 75+ age group.

Space for calculation

_____ % **1**

Marks

8. **(continued)**

(*e*)   (i)   Type 1 diabetics are unable to produce enough insulin.

Where is insulin produced in the body?

_____

1

(ii)   Describe the role of insulin in the liver.

_____

_____

1

[Turn over

Marks

9. The diagram below represents the passage of information through memory.

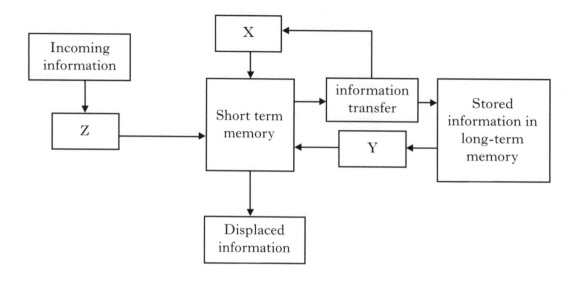

(*a*)   (i)   Identify processes X, Y and Z.

X _____

Y _____

Z _____   **2**

(ii)   State **two** forms of information which can enter short term memory.

1 _____

2 _____   **1**

(iii) Describe how contextual cues help recall from long-term memory.

_____

_____

_____   **1**

(*b*)   A student had to learn her SQA candidate number which contained 9 digits. She was advised to use chunking to help her memorise it.

Explain why the process of chunking would help her memorise this number.

_____

_____

_____   **1**

DO NOT WRITE IN THIS MARGIN

Marks

9. (continued)

(*c*) (i) Patients with Alzheimer's disease find it difficult to form new memories. Which part of the brain is affected by Alzheimer's disease?

______________________________ **1**

(ii) Name the receptor thought to be important in the process of memory storage.

______________________________ **1**

[Turn over

DO N
WRIT
THI
MARC

Marks

10. An investigation was carried out into the effects of organisation on improving the recall of information.

Four students were each asked to look at a card containing 25 words organised into a branching diagram. The card is shown below.

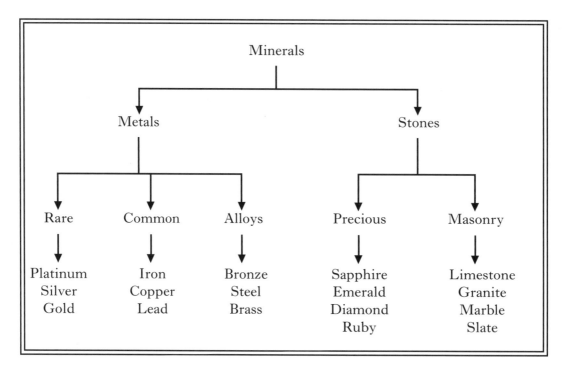

The card was removed after three minutes and each student had to write down as many words as he or she could recall. A score out of 25 was recorded for each student and these were added together to give a total score out of 100 for the group. The procedure was repeated twice. Each time the students were given cards containing 25 different words also organised into branching diagrams. Another group of four students took part in the control for this investigation. The words on their cards were not organised.

The results are shown in the table below.

| | Total number of words recalled (out of 100) | | | |
Student Group	1st card	2nd card	3rd card	average
Experimental	75	78	72	
Control	53	57	55	

(a) Complete the table by calculating the average number of words recalled by each student group.

Space for calculation

1

DO NOT
WRITE IN
THIS
MARGIN

Marks

10. **(continued)**

(b) In what way would the content of the control cards be

similar to the experimental cards? _____

_____

different from the experimental cards? _____

_____   1

(c) Suggest **two** variables, not already mentioned in the description of this investigation, which would have to be kept constant to ensure that a valid comparison could be made between the two groups.

1 _____

2 _____   2

(d) State a conclusion that can be drawn from the results.

_____

_____   1

(e) How could the reliability of the results of this investigation be improved?

_____

_____   1

(f) At the start of the investigation the students were told that the person in each group who recalled most words would be given a prize.

Why did the design of this investigation include a prize?

_____

_____   1

(g) In a further investigation into recall, students were given the same card to memorise on three successive occasions.

Predict what would happen to the number of words recalled on each successive attempt. Explain your prediction.

Prediction _____

Explanation _____   1

[Turn over

Marks

11. The diagram below shows a motor neurone and its junction with skeletal muscle tissue.

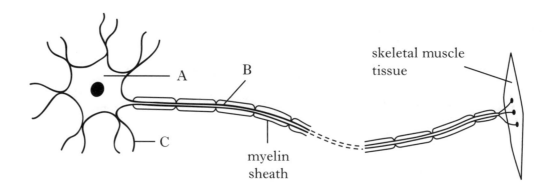

(a) Name the parts of the neurone labelled A, B and C on the diagram.

A _____

B _____

C _____   **2**

(b) Neurotransmitters bind to receptors on skeletal muscle tissue triggering contraction.

(i) Name **two** neurotransmitters.

1 _____

2 _____   **1**

(ii) Explain why the release of neurotransmitter into a synaptic cleft may sometimes fail to trigger muscle contraction.

_____

_____   **1**

(iii) Name the structural proteins in skeletal muscle tissue and describe how they interact to bring about muscle contraction.

Proteins _____   **1**

Description _____

_____   **1**

DO NOT WRITE IN THIS MARGIN

Marks

11. (continued)

(*c*) (i) State the importance of the myelin sheath in the transmission of impulses.

____

____ **1**

(ii) Post-natal myelination is necessary for a child to go through the sequence of developmental stages leading to walking.

What term describes this sequence of developmental stages?

____________________ **1**

[Turn over

DO N
WRIT
TH
MAR

Marks

12. The table below shows the biomass of cod and herring stocks in the North Sea between 1967 and 2004.

The biomass figures are estimates of the total mass of each species present in the North Sea during that year. The critical biomass indicates the mass of each species that must be maintained to prevent it becoming endangered.

Fish species	Estimated Biomass per year (thousand tonnes)					Critical biomass (thousand tonnes)
	1967	1980	1990	2000	2004	
Cod	235	170	75	50	45	150
Herring	920	130	1170	825	1890	1300

(*a*) (i) Construct a line graph to illustrate the data for cod.

(Additional graph paper, if required, can be found on *Page thirty-four*)

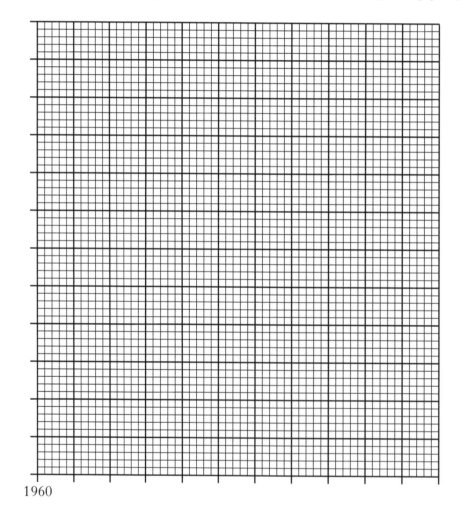

1960

2

(ii) For how many years between 1967 and 2004 was the cod endangered?

Space for calculation

_____ years   **1**

DO NOT WRITE IN THIS MARGIN

Marks

12. (continued)

(*b*) (i) Calculate the percentage increase in the estimated biomass of herring between 1980 and 1990.

Space for calculation

________ **1**

(ii) Suggest a reason for the increase in herring biomass between 1980 and 1990.

____

________________________________ **1**

(*c*) What term describes the maximum size of a population which can be sustained by a particular environment?

________________________________ **1**

[Turn over for Section C on *Page thirty*

Marks

SECTION C

Both questions in this section should be attempted.

Note that each question contains a choice.

Questions 1 and 2 should be attempted on the blank pages which follow.

Supplementary sheets, if required, may be obtained from the invigilator.

Labelled diagrams may be used where appropriate.

1. Answer **either** A **or** B.

    A. Give an account of communication under the following headings:

    (i) the use of language;   **4**

    (ii) non-verbal communication.   **6**

    OR   **(10)**

    B. Give an account of the environmental effects of an increasing human population under the following headings:

    (i) deforestation;   **6**

    (ii) increasing atmospheric methane levels.   **4**

                                                                           (10)

In question 2, ONE mark is available for coherence and ONE mark is available for relevance.

2. Answer **either** A **or** B.

    A. Discuss factors that affect enzyme activity.   **(10)**

    OR

    B. Discuss the production and use of ATP in the body.   **(10)**

[END OF QUESTION PAPER]

SPACE FOR ANSWERS

SPACE FOR ANSWERS

ADDITIONAL GRAPH FOR QUESTION 12(*a*)(i)

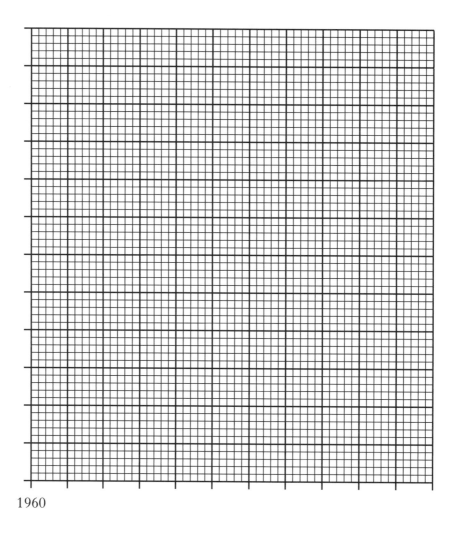

1960

[BLANK PAGE]

FOR OFFICIAL USE

Total for
Sections B & C

X009/12/02

NATIONAL   WEDNESDAY, 23 MAY   HUMAN BIOLOGY
QUALIFICATIONS   1.00 PM – 3.30 PM   HIGHER
2012

Fill in these boxes and read what is printed below.

Full name of centre   Town

Forename(s)   Surname

Date of birth
Day   Month   Year   Scottish candidate number   Number of seat

SECTION A—Questions 1–30

Instructions for completion of Section A are given on page two.

For this section of the examination you must use an **HB pencil**.

SECTIONS B AND C

1 (a) All questions should be attempted.

   (b) It should be noted that in **Section C** questions 1 and 2 each contain a choice.

2 The questions may be answered in any order but all answers are to be written in the spaces provided in this answer book, **and must be written clearly and legibly in ink**.

3 Additional space for answers will be found at the end of the book. If further space is required, supplementary sheets may be obtained from the Invigilator and should be inserted inside the **front** cover of this book.

4 The numbers of questions must be clearly inserted with any answers written in the additional space.

5 Rough work, if any should be necessary, should be written in this book and then scored through when the fair copy has been written. If further space is required a supplementary sheet for rough work may be obtained from the Invigilator.

6 Before leaving the examination room you must give this book to the Invigilator. If you do not, you may lose all the marks for this paper.

Read carefully

1   Check that the answer sheet provided is for **Human Biology Higher (Section A)**.

2   For this section of the examination you must use an **HB pencil**, and where necessary, an eraser.

3   Check that the answer sheet you have been given has **your name**, **date of birth**, **SCN** (Scottish Candidate Number) and **Centre Name** printed on it.

   Do not change any of these details.

4   If any of this information is wrong, tell the Invigilator immediately.

5   If this information is correct, **print** your name and seat number in the boxes provided.

6   The answer to each question is **either** A, B, C or D. Decide what your answer is, then, using your pencil, put a horizontal line in the space provided (see sample question below).

7   There is **only one correct** answer to each question.

8   Any rough working should be done on the question paper or the rough working sheet, not on your answer sheet.

9   At the end of the examination, put the **answer sheet for Section A inside the front cover of this answer book**.

Sample Question

The digestive enzyme pepsin is most active in the

A   stomach

B   mouth

C   duodenum

D   pancreas.

The correct answer is **A**—stomach. The answer **A** has been clearly marked in **pencil** with a horizontal line (see below).

A   B   C   D

Changing an answer

If you decide to change your answer, carefully erase your first answer and, using your pencil, fill in the answer you want. The answer below has been changed to **D**.

A   B   C   D

SECTION A

All questions in this section should be attempted.

Answers should be given on the separate answer sheet provided.

1. The diagram below shows some protein filaments in muscle. Which protein is labelled with the letter P?

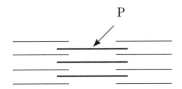

A   Actin

B   Adenine

C   Adenosine

D   Myosin

2. The following cell components are involved in the synthesis and secretion of an enzyme.

   1   Golgi apparatus

   2   Ribosome

   3   Cytoplasm

   4   Endoplasmic reticulum

   Which of the following identifies correctly the route an amino acid molecule would follow as an enzyme is synthesised and secreted?

   A   3 2 1 4

   B   2 4 3 1

   C   3 2 4 1

   D   3 4 2 1

3. How many adenine molecules are present in a DNA molecule of 4000 bases, if 20% of the base molecules are cytosine?

   A   400

   B   600

   C   800

   D   1200

4. The following statements refer to respiration:

   1   Carbon dioxide is released

   2   Occurs during aerobic respiration

   3   The end product is pyruvic acid

   4   The end product is lactic acid

   Which statements refer to glycolysis?

   A   1 and 4

   B   2 and 3

   C   1 and 3

   D   2 and 4

5. The diagram below represents a cross-section of a membrane magnified 2 million times.

16 mm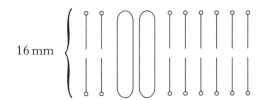

   What is the actual width of the membrane?

   $1\,nm = 1 \times 10^{-6}\,mm$

   A $1 \cdot 6\,nm$

   B $3 \cdot 2\,nm$

   C $8 \cdot 0\,nm$

   D $16 \cdot 0\,nm$

6. During the manufacture of protein in a cell, the synthesis of mRNA occurs in the

   A   nucleus

   B   ribosomes

   C   Golgi body

   D   endoplasmic reticulum.

[Turn over

7. The following diagram shows some stages in the synthesis of part of a polypeptide.

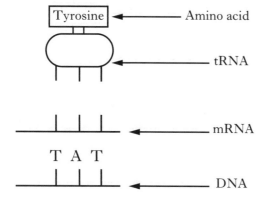

Identify the triplet codes for the amino acid tyrosine.

	On mRNA	On tRNA
A	ATA	UAU
B	UAU	AUA
C	AUA	UAU
D	ATA	TAT

8. Visking tubing is selectively permeable. In the experiment shown below, to demonstrate osmosis, the following results were obtained.

Initial mass of visking tubing + contents   = 10·0 g

Mass of visking tubing + contents after experiment   = 8·2 g

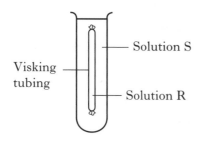

The results shown would be obtained when

A   R is a 5% salt solution and S is a 10% salt solution

B   R is a 10% salt solution and S is a 5% salt solution

C   R is a 10% salt solution and S is water

D   R is a 5% salt solution and S is water.

9. In the formation of gametes when does DNA replication occur?

A   At the separation of chromatids

B   As homologous chromosomes pair

C   Before the start of meiosis

D   At the end of the first meiotic division

10. Identical twins can result from

A   a haploid egg fertilised by a single sperm

B   a haploid egg fertilised by two identical sperm

C   a diploid egg fertilised by a single sperm

D   two haploid eggs fertilised by two identical sperm.

11. The diagram below represents a stage in the division of a cell.

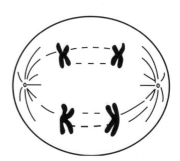

Which line of the table identifies correctly the type of division and the number of chromosomes?

	Type of division	Number of chromosomes
A	mitosis	8
B	mitosis	4
C	meiosis	8
D	meiosis	4

12. Phenylketonuria is caused by a single autosomal gene.

A man and a woman, who are unaffected, have an affected child.

What is the probability that their next child will be affected?

A 25%

B 50%

C 75%

D 100%

13. The offspring from a mother who is homozygous for blood group A and a father who is heterozygous for blood group B, will have a blood group which is

A AB or A

B AB or B

C A or B

D A or O.

14. A function of the interstitial cells in the testes is to produce

A sperm

B testosterone

C seminal fluid

D follicle stimulating hormone (FSH).

15. Which of the following is the sequence of events following fertilisation?

A Cleavage ⟶ Differentiation ⟶ Implantation

B Implantation ⟶ Differentiation ⟶ Cleavage

C Differentiation ⟶ Implantation ⟶ Cleavage

D Cleavage ⟶ Implantation ⟶ Differentiation

16. The graph below shows the changes which occur in a body's food stores during four weeks of food deprivation.

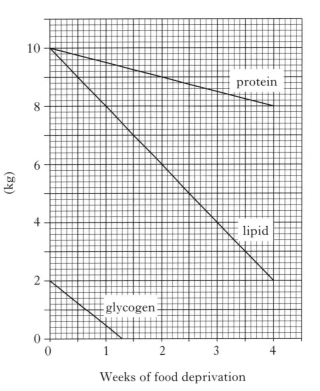

Weeks of food deprivation

Which of the following conclusions can be drawn from the graph?

A The glycogen food store decreases at the fastest rate during week one.

B Between weeks three and four the body gains most energy from protein.

C Each food store decreases at a constant rate during week one.

D Between weeks one and four the body only gains energy from lipid and protein.

[Turn over

17. The graph below shows the growth in length of a human fetus before birth.

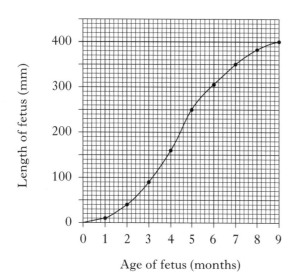

Age of fetus (months)

What is the percentage increase in length of the fetus during the final 4 months of pregnancy?

A   33·3

B   60·0

C   62·5

D   150·0

18. The sperm counts of a sample of men taken between 1940 and 2000 are shown in the graph below.

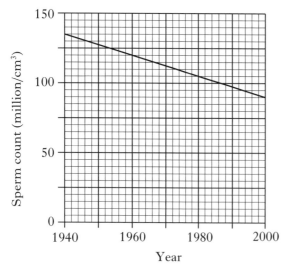

Year

What is the average reduction in sperm count per year?

A   0·67 million/cm^3/year

B   0·75 million/cm^3/year

C   0·92 million/cm^3/year

D   45 million/cm^3/year

19. The effect on the kidney of a high concentration of antidiuretic hormone (ADH) in the blood is to

A   increase tubule permeability which increases water reabsorption

B   decrease tubule permeability which prevents excessive water loss

C   increase glomerular filtration rate which increases urine production

D   decrease glomerular filtration rate which reduces urine production.

20. Compared to the blood in the renal artery, the blood in the renal vein has a higher concentration of

A   oxygen

B   carbon dioxide

C   glucose

D   urea.

21. The graph below records the body temperature of a woman during an investigation in which her arm was immersed in warm water for 5 minutes.

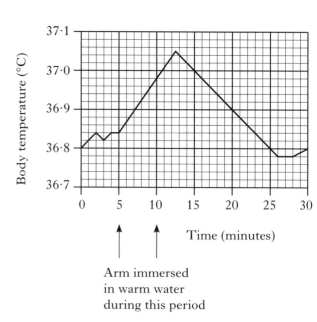

Time (minutes)

Arm immersed
in warm water
during this period

By how much did the temperature of her body vary during the 30 minutes of the investigation?

A   2·7 °C

B   0·27 °C

C   2·5 °C

D   0·25 °C

22. The flow chart below shows how the concentration of glucose in the blood is regulated.

Blood glucose concentration rises ⟶ Pancreas secretes less of compound X and more of compound Y ⟶ Liver converts glucose to insoluble carbohydrate ⟶ Blood glucose concentration falls

Which line identifies correctly the compounds X and Y?

	Compound X	Compound Y
A	glycogen	insulin
B	insulin	glycogen
C	glucagon	insulin
D	insulin	glucagon

23. The somatic nervous system controls the

   A   skeletal muscles

   B   heart and blood vessels

   C   endocrine glands

   D   muscular wall of the gut.

24. The following is a list of body parts:

   1   tongue

   2   eyebrows

   3   hands

   4   eyes.

   Which of these body parts can be used in non-verbal communication?

   A   3 only

   B   2 and 4 only

   C   2, 3 and 4 only

   D   1, 2, 3 and 4

25. An athlete has a much better chance of achieving a "personal best" time in a race rather than in training because of

   A   internalisation

   B   deindividuation

   C   identification

   D   social facilitation.

26. The rewarding of patterns of behaviour which approximate to desired behaviour is called

   A   generalisation

   B   discrimination

   C   extinction

   D   shaping.

27. In the nitrogen cycle, which of the following processes is carried out by nitrifying bacteria?

   The conversion of

   A   nitrate to ammonia

   B   nitrogen gas to ammonia

   C   ammonia to nitrate

   D   nitrogen gas to nitrate.

[Turn over

28. The graph below shows the time taken by a student to complete a finger maze, over a number of trials, and the number of errors at each trial.

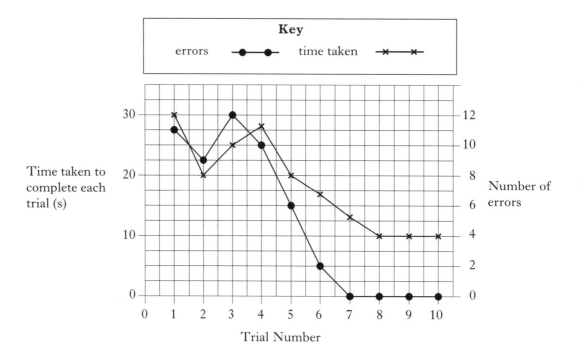

Which of the following statements is correct?

A   The fastest time to complete the maze correctly is 4 seconds.

B   The time taken at trial 5 is 20 seconds.

C   When the number of errors is 10, the time taken is 25 seconds.

D   The number of errors decreased with each subsequent trial.

29. The bar chart below shows the percentage loss in yield of four organically grown crops, as a result of the effects of weeds, disease and insects.

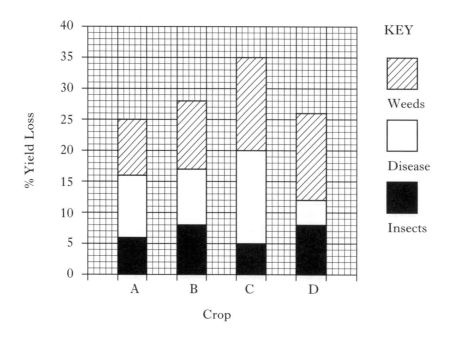

Which crop is likely to show the greatest increase in yield if herbicides and insecticides were applied?

30. The graph below shows how the UK diet changed between 1988 and 1998.

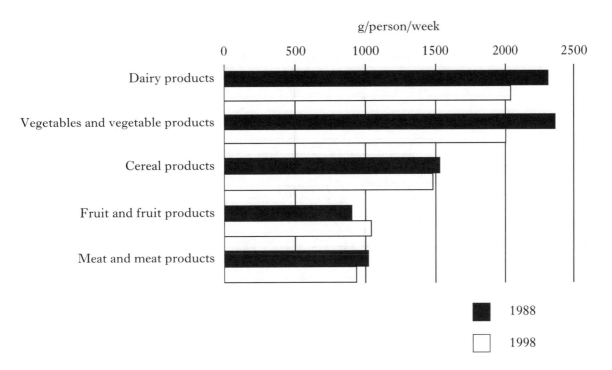

Which of the following conclusions can be drawn from the data?

A   People ate more food in 1998 than in 1988.

B   People ate less food in 1998 than in 1988.

C   People ate a greater variety of food in 1998 than in 1988.

D   People ate a lesser variety of food in 1998 than in 1988.

**Candidates are reminded that the answer sheet MUST be returned
INSIDE the front cover of this answer booklet.**

[Turn over for Section B on *page ten*

Marks

SECTION B

All questions in this section should be attempted.

All answers must be written clearly and legibly in ink.

1. The diagram below shows a cell from the lining of a kidney tubule.

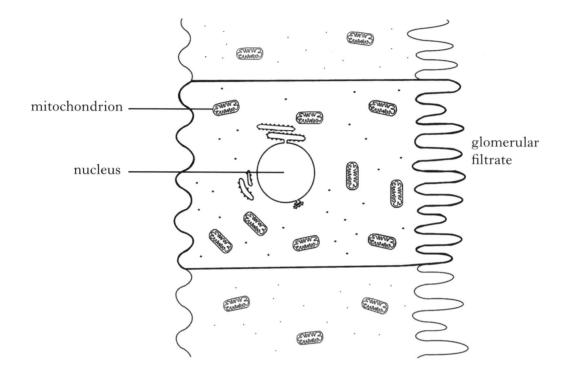

mitochondrion

nucleus

glomerular
filtrate

(a) This cell is adapted to reabsorb substances from the glomerular filtrate by active transport.

(i) What is meant by active transport?

_____

_____   1

(ii) Describe how this cell is adapted for active transport.

_____

_____   1

(iii) Explain how this cell is adapted for reabsorption.

_____

_____   1

Marks

1. **(continued)**

(b) Name the component of the membrane which is involved in active transport.

_____   1

(c) The diagram below shows one of the mitochondria from this kidney tubule cell in greater detail.

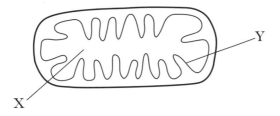

(i) Complete the table below by naming the labelled regions of the mitochondrion and the stage of respiration that occurs there

Region	Name	Respiration stage
X		
Y		

2

(ii) Suggest how the structure of a mitochondrion from a less active cell would differ from the structure of the mitochondrion shown.

Give a reason for your answer.

Structural difference _____

_____

Reason _____

_____   1

[Turn over

Marks

2. The diagram below shows how the immune system responds to a polio virus in a vaccine.

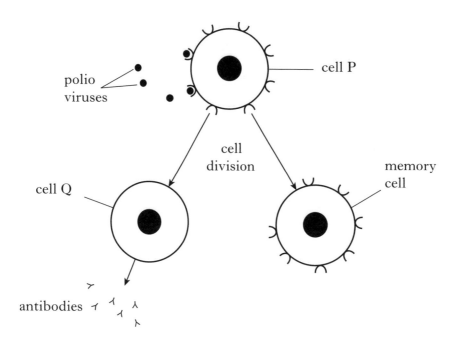

(a) What type of immunological response involves the production of antibodies?

_____   1

(b) (i) Name cell Q.

_____   1

  (ii) Describe **two** functions of cell P that are shown in the diagram.

  1 _____

  2 _____   1

(c) Describe the role of memory cells in the immune system.

_____

_____   1

Marks

DO NOT
WRITE
IN THIS
MARGIN

2. **(continued)**

(*d*) Explain why vaccination against polio would not provide immunity against the measles virus.

_____

_____ 1

(*e*) In an emergency, ready-made antibodies can be injected into an individual.

(i) Name the type of immunity that this gives.

_____ 1

(ii) State **one** advantage and **one** disadvantage of this type of immunity.

Advantage _____

_____

Disadvantage _____

_____ 2

[Turn over

Marks

3. Duchenne's muscular dystrophy is an inherited condition in which muscle fibres gradually degenerate.

The condition is sex-linked and caused by a recessive allele.

The family tree below shows the inheritance of the condition through three generations of a family.

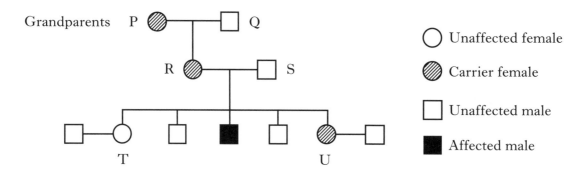

(*a*)   (i)   Using the symbols **D** and **d** to represent the alleles, state the genotypes of individuals R and S.

R _____   S _____   1

(ii)   What percentage of the grandsons have muscular dystrophy?

_____   1

(iii)   Sisters T and U each go on to have a son.

For each sister, state the percentage chance of her son having muscular dystrophy.

Son of T _____   Son of U _____   1

DO NOT WRITE IN THIS MARGIN

Marks

3. (continued)

(*b*) In humans there is a gene which codes for the essential muscle protein dystrophin.

When this gene is altered, dystrophin is not produced.

An individual with Duchenne's muscular dystrophy cannot make dystrophin.

(i) What general term is used to describe a gene alteration?

______________________________ **1**

(ii) How might the structure of the gene which codes for dystrophin be altered?

____

____ **1**

(iii) Why does this altered gene fail to produce dystrophin?

____

____ **1**

(*c*) Where conditions such as Duchenne's muscular dystrophy exist in a family, the family history can be used to determine the genotypes of its individual members.

What term is used for this process?

__________________________________ **1**

[Turn over

Marks

4. (*a*) Photographic film consists of a clear sheet of plastic coated with chemicals that give it a dark appearance. The chemicals are stuck to the plastic by the protein gelatine.

An investigation was carried out using photographic film and the enzyme trypsin which digests protein.

A piece of photographic film was placed in a test tube containing a solution of trypsin, as shown in **Figure 1** below.

The time taken for the film to turn clear was measured.

The procedure was then repeated using different concentrations of trypsin solution.

The results of the investigation are shown in **Table 1** below.

Figure 1

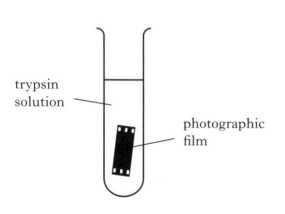

Table 1

Trypsin concentration (%)	*Time taken for film to clear* (s)
1	112
2	102
3	93
4	84
5	84
6	84

(i) Explain why the photographic film turns clear in this investigation.

_____

_____   **1**

(ii) List **two** variables which would have to be kept constant throughout the investigation.

1 _____

2 _____   **2**

(iii) How could the reliability of the results of this investigation be improved?

_____

_____   **1**

Marks

4. (*a*) (**continued**)

(iv) Plot a line graph to illustrate the results of the investigation.

(Additional graph paper, if required, can be found on *Page thirty-six*)

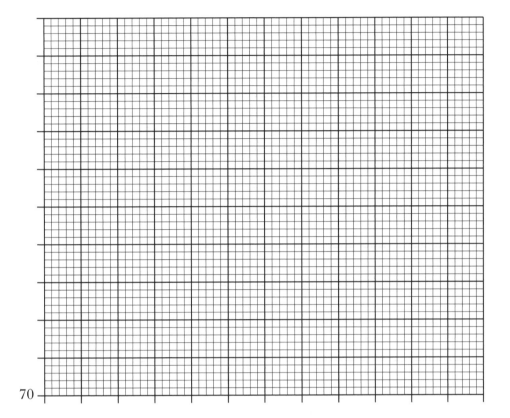

70

2

(v) Explain why the time taken for the film to clear changed as trypsin concentration increased from 1% to 4%.

_____

_____ 1

(vi) Suggest why there was no change in the time taken to clear the film at trypsin concentrations above 4%.

_____

_____ 1

[Turn over

Marks

4. (continued)

(*b*) An inactive form of trypsin called trypsinogen is produced and released from the pancreas. Trypsinogen is then converted to trypsin by another enzyme.

  (i) In which part of the digestive system does activation of trypsin occur?

  _____   **1**

  (ii) Why are some enzymes such as trypsin produced in an inactive form?

  _____

  _____   **1**

  (iii) Apart from other enzymes, name another type of molecule that can act as an enzyme activator.

  _____   **1**

Marks

5. The diagram shows a section through the heart and two areas, X and Y, which help to coordinate the heart beat.

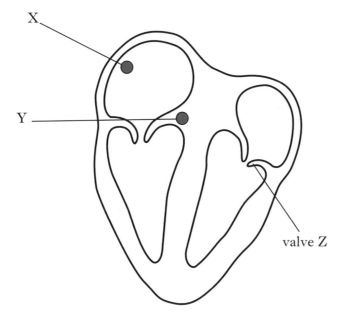

(a) (i) Name structures X and Y.

X _____

Y _____   1

(ii) Electrical impulses travel from X to Y.

What is happening to the heart during this time?

_____   1

(iii) **Draw** arrows on the diagram to show the pathway taken by electrical impulses produced by structure Y.   1

(b) (i) Name valve Z.

_____   1

(ii) During which stage of the cardiac cycle is valve Z closed?

_____   1

[Turn over

Marks

6. The graph below shows the concentrations of two ovarian hormones in a woman's blood during her menstrual cycle.

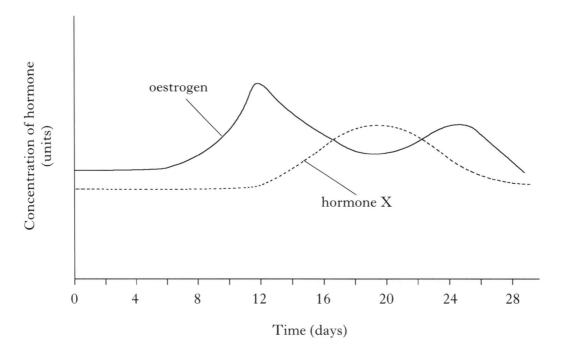

(a) Name hormone X.

_____   1

(b) What effect does oestrogen have on the following structures?

   (i) The uterus between days 4 and 12 in the cycle.

   _____

   _____   1

   (ii) The pituitary gland on day 12 of the cycle.

   _____

   _____   1

(c) Describe **one** way in which the graph would be different if the woman became pregnant during this cycle.

   _____

   _____   1

Marks

6. **(continued)**

   (*d*) The diagrams below show sections through two structures found in the ovary
   at different times in the menstrual cycle.

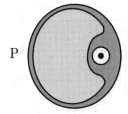   

   (i) Name structures P and Q.

   P _____   Q _____   **1**

   (ii) What key event in the menstrual cycle occurs before P develops into Q?

   _____   **1**

   [Turn over

DO N
WRI
IN T
MARC

Marks

7. The graph below shows changes that occurred in a man's breathing when he inhaled air containing different concentrations of carbon dioxide.

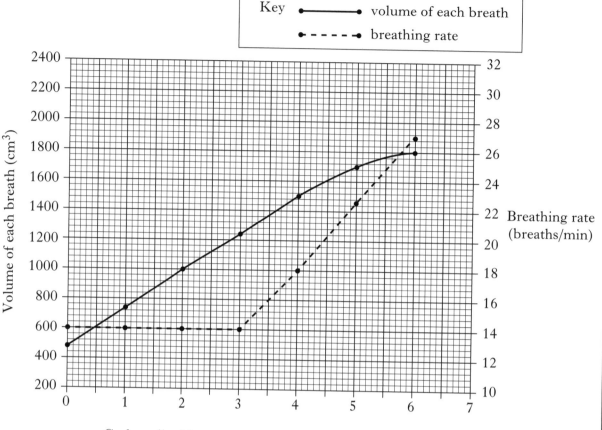

Carbon dioxide concentration of inhaled air (%)

(*a*) Use data from the graph to describe the changes that occurred in the man's breathing when the carbon dioxide concentration of inhaled air increased from 0 to 3%.

_____

_____

_____

_____

_____   **2**

(*b*) What was the man's breathing rate when the volume of each breath was 1500 cm³?

_____ breaths/min   **1**

DO NOT
WRITE
IN THIS
MARGIN

Marks

7. **(continued)**

(c) Calculate the volume of air inhaled in one minute when the carbon dioxide concentration was 2%.

Space for calculation

_____ cm^3 1

(d) (i) Predict what the volume of each breath would have been if a carbon dioxide concentration of 7% had been used.

Volume of each breath   _____   1

(ii) Suggest why the increase in the volume of each breath becomes less at carbon dioxide concentrations above 4%.

_____

_____   1

(e) On average there is 0·04% carbon dioxide in inhaled air and 4% carbon dioxide in exhaled air.

Explain why this change in carbon dioxide concentration occurs.

_____

_____   1

[Turn over

Marks

8. The diagram below represents the liver and some associated structures.

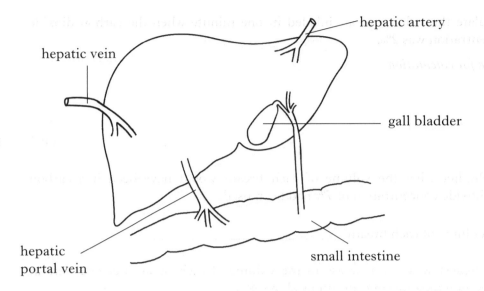

(a) **Draw** arrows beside each of the **three** blood vessels to show the direction of blood flow.   **1**

(b)   (i) Name the liquid stored in the gall bladder.

_____   **1**

(ii) State **one** function of this liquid and explain how it aids digestion.

Function_____

_____   **1**

Explanation_____

_____   **1**

(c) Name **one** substance that is stored in the liver.

_____   **1**

Marks

9. The image below shows a vertical section through a human brain.

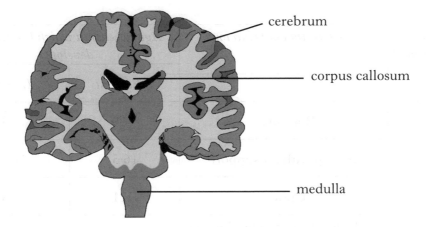

cerebrum

corpus callosum

medulla

(a) Explain how the maximum number of interconnections between neurones is achieved within the cerebrum.

_____

_____

_____   **2**

(b) What is the function of the corpus callosum?

_____

_____   **1**

(c)   (i) Which division of the nervous system is linked to the medulla?

_____   **1**

    (ii) Describe how this division of the nervous system controls heart rate.

_____

_____   **1**

[Turn over

Marks

10. The information in the table below refers to the development of walking by infant boys.

Stage of development	Description of behaviour	Age (weeks) at which behaviour develops	
		Earliest	Latest
1	Rolls over	9	23
2	Sits up without support	16·5	32·5
3	Crawls	21	38
4	Pulls up and stands holding on to furniture	23	43
5	Walks holding on to furniture	28·5	49
6	Stands unsupported	35·5	54
7	Walks alone	44·5	57·5

(a) Assuming a normal pattern of distribution, predict by what age 50% of boys would be expected to walk alone.

Space for calculation

_____   **1**

(b) Identify all the stages in the development of walking that boys could be at when they are 36 weeks old.

Tick the correct boxes

| 1 | | 2 | | 3 | | 4 | | 5 | | 6 | | 7 | |

1

(c) Suggest **two** reasons why a boy might still only be crawling when, at the same age, his elder brother could stand unsupported.

1 _____

2 _____   **1**

DO NOT WRITE IN THIS MARGIN

Marks

10. (continued)

(*d*) (i) What term describes the development of a behaviour which follows a set sequence of stages?

______________________ **1**

(ii) Describe the change which occurs in the nervous system that allows children to go through the stages of development leading to walking.

______________________ **1**

[Turn over

Marks

11. An investigation was carried out into the effect that the meaning of words has on the ability to recall them from short and long-term memory.

Two groups of people were each shown lists of five words for 30 seconds.

Group 1 was shown words with related meanings while group 2 was shown words with unrelated meanings.

> List of words with related meanings – *large, big, great, huge, wide.*
> List of words with unrelated meanings – *late, cheap, rare, bright, rough.*

Immediately after the 30 seconds, the people in both groups were asked to write down, in the correct order, the words that they had been shown.

Everyone was then asked to read a book for one hour and told that they would be asked questions about it afterwards.

Instead, after the hour had passed, everyone was again asked to write down, in the correct order, the words that they had been shown in their original list.

The results of the investigation are shown in the table below.

Group	Meaning of words shown	Correct responses immediately after reading the words (%)	Correct responses after reading the book for one hour (%)
1	related	96	54
2	unrelated	96	78

(a) List **two** ways in which the investigators could minimise variation between the two groups of people.

1 _____

2 _____   1

(b) What aspect of memory explains the high percentage of correct responses immediately after reading the words?

_____

_____   1

(c) Suggest why the groups were asked to read a book during the investigation.

_____

_____   1

DO NOT WRITE IN THIS MARGIN

Marks

11. (continued)

(*d*) State **two** conclusions that can be drawn from the results of this investigation.

1 ______________________________________

____

2 ______________________________________

______________________________________ **2**

[Turn over

Marks

12. The diagram below shows the changes that affect the population of a country as it undergoes development.

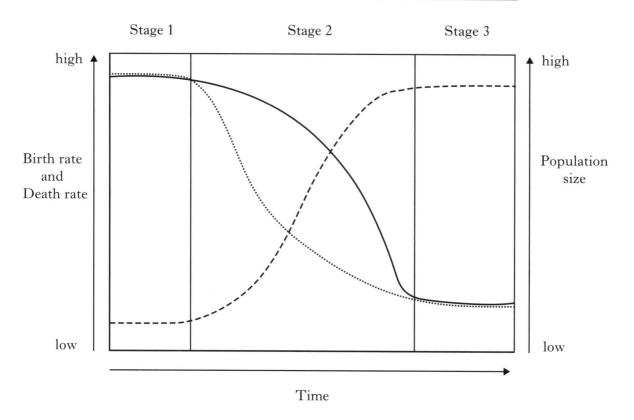

(*a*) (i) Describe the country's birth rate at stage 2 and stage 3 during its development.

_____

_____   1

(ii) Use information from the diagram to explain why the population size increases rapidly and then starts to level off during stage 2.

_____

_____

_____

_____   2

Marks

12. (a) (continued)

(iii) Suggest **two** factors which may contribute to the change in the death rate during stage 2.

1 _____

2 _____   1

(b) The increasing world population requires an increased supply of food.

(i) Pesticides are chemicals which can be used to increase food supply. However, their use can lead to instability in food webs.

Explain this effect.

_____

_____

_____   1

(ii) Other chemicals, such as fertilisers, are also used to increase food production.

Name another method of increasing food production that does not involve chemicals.

_____   1

(c) When fertilisers are used in agriculture they can pollute rivers and lochs causing algal blooms.

(i) What is an algal bloom?

_____

_____   1

(ii) Describe the effects an algal bloom might have on a loch.

_____

_____

_____

_____

_____   2

[Turn over for Section C on *Page thirty-two*

DO N
WRI
IN T
MAR

SECTION C

Marks

Both questions in this section should be attempted.

Note that each question contains a choice.

Questions 1 and 2 should be attempted on the blank pages which follow.

Supplementary sheets, if required, may be obtained from the Invigilator.

Labelled diagrams may be used where appropriate.

1. Answer **either** A **or** B.

    A   Give an account of the carbon cycle under the following headings:

       (i) natural uptake and release of carbon;   **4**

      (ii) disruption of the carbon cycle by human activities.   **6**

                                                          (10)

   OR

    B   Give an account of the nervous system under the following headings:

       (i) the role of neurotransmitters at the synapse;   **6**

      (ii) converging and diverging neural pathways.   **4**

                                                            (10)

In question 2, ONE mark is available for coherence and ONE mark is available for relevance.

2. Answer **either** A **or** B.

    A   Describe the exchange of substances between plasma and body cells.   **(10)**

   OR

    B   Describe involuntary mechanisms of temperature control.   **(10)**

[END OF QUESTION PAPER]

SPACE FOR ANSWERS

DO N
WRI
IN T
MAR

SPACE FOR ANSWERS

Page thirty-four

SPACE FOR ANSWERS

SPACE FOR ANSWERS

ADDITIONAL GRAPH FOR QUESTION 4(*a*) (iv)

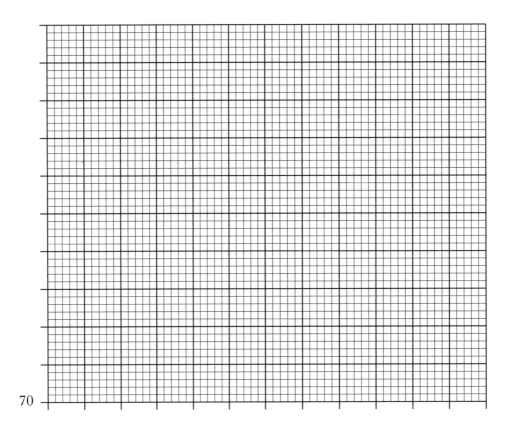

70

HIGHER

2013

[BLANK PAGE]

FOR OFFICIAL USE

Total for
Sections B & C

X009/12/02

NATIONAL
QUALIFICATIONS
2013

WEDNESDAY, 15 MAY
1.00 PM – 3.30 PM

HUMAN BIOLOGY
HIGHER

Fill in these boxes and read what is printed below.

Full name of centre

Town

Forename(s)

Surname

Date of birth

Day	Month	Year	Scottish candidate number	Number of seat

SECTION A—Questions 1–30 (30 marks)

Instructions for completion of Section A are given on page two.

For this section of the examination you must use an **HB pencil**.

SECTIONS B AND C (100 marks)

1 (a) All questions should be attempted.

   (b) It should be noted that in **Section C** questions 1 and 2 each contain a choice.

2 The questions may be answered in any order but all answers are to be written in the spaces provided in this answer book, **and must be written clearly and legibly in ink**.

3 Additional space for answers will be found at the end of the book. If further space is required, supplementary sheets may be obtained from the Invigilator and should be inserted inside the **front** cover of this book.

4 The numbers of questions must be clearly inserted with any answers written in the additional space.

5 Rough work, if any should be necessary, should be written in this book and then scored through when the fair copy has been written. If further space is required a supplementary sheet for rough work may be obtained from the Invigilator.

6 Before leaving the examination room you must give this book to the Invigilator. If you do not, you may lose all the marks for this paper.

Read carefully

1   Check that the answer sheet provided is for **Human Biology Higher (Section A)**.

2   For this section of the examination you must use an **HB pencil**, and where necessary, an eraser.

3   Check that the answer sheet you have been given has **your name**, **date of birth**, **SCN** (Scottish Candidate Number) and **Centre Name** printed on it.

Do not change any of these details.

4   If any of this information is wrong, tell the Invigilator immediately.

5   If this information is correct, **print** your name and seat number in the boxes provided.

6   The answer to each question is **either** A, B, C or D. Decide what your answer is, then, using your pencil, put a horizontal line in the space provided (see sample question below).

7   There is **only one correct** answer to each question.

8   Any rough working should be done on the question paper or the rough working sheet, not on your answer sheet.

9   At the end of the examination, put the **answer sheet for Section A inside the front cover of this answer book**.

Sample Question

The digestive enzyme pepsin is most active in the

A   stomach

B   mouth

C   duodenum

D   pancreas.

The correct answer is **A**—stomach. The answer **A** has been clearly marked in **pencil** with a horizontal line (see below).

A   B   C   D

Changing an answer

If you decide to change your answer, carefully erase your first answer and, using your pencil, fill in the answer you want. The answer below has been changed to **D**.

A   B   C   D

SECTION A

All questions in this section should be attempted.

Answers should be given on the separate answer sheet provided.

1. Actin is a type of protein involved in

A   contraction of muscles

B   production of lactic acid

C   protection against infection

D   production of cell membranes.

2. Which line in the table below describes correctly the bonds that create the shape of a protein at a particular stage of its formation?

	Stage of formation	Shape of protein	Bonds
A	primary structure	chain	hydrogen
B	secondary structure	helix	hydrogen
C	primary structure	helix	peptide
D	secondary structure	chain	peptide

3. If ten percent of the bases in a molecule of DNA are adenine, what is the ratio of adenine to guanine in the same molecule?

A   1:1

B   1:2

C   1:3

D   1:4

4. The table below contains statements which may be **True** or **False** with regard to DNA replication and mRNA synthesis.

Which line in the table is correct?

	Statement	DNA Replication	mRNA synthesis
A	Occurs in the nucleus	True	False
B	Involved in protein synthesis	True	True
C	Requires free nucleotides	True	False
D	Involves specific base pairing	True	True

5. The diagram below shows the transmission of the gene for albinism.

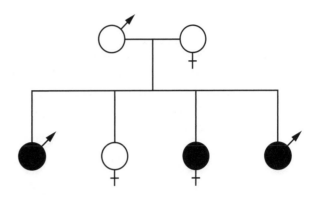

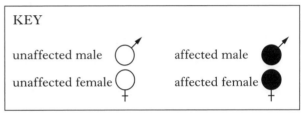

KEY		
unaffected male		affected male
unaffected female		affected female

This condition is inherited as a characteristic which is

A   dominant and not sex-linked

B   recessive and not sex-linked

C   dominant and sex-linked

D   recessive and sex-linked.

6. Two alleles of a gene code for different proteins. Both proteins are present in the heterozygote. This is an example of

A   co-dominance

B   sex-linkage

C   polygenic inheritance

D   complete dominance.

[Turn over

7. Which of the following are all examples of polygenic characteristics?

    A   Hand span, height and skin colour

    B   Blood group, height and foot size

    C   Hand span, tongue rolling and weight

    D   Blood group, foot size and skin colour

8. A substitution mutation results in a triplet of bases TTC being changed to TCC. The amino acid lysine is coded for by TTC and arginine by TCC.

    The effect of such a mutation on the resultant protein would be that

    A   arginine replaces lysine throughout the protein

    B   arginine replaces lysine at one position in the protein

    C   lysine replaces arginine throughout the protein

    D   lysine replaces arginine at one position in the protein.

9. The graph below shows changes in the concentration of hormones X and Y in the blood during the menstrual cycle.

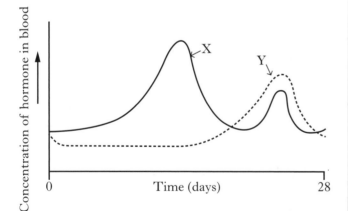

    Which of the following correctly identifies hormones X and Y?

	Hormone X	Hormone Y
A	LH	Oestrogen
B	Oestrogen	FSH
C	Oestrogen	Progesterone
D	Progesterone	Oestrogen

10. Changes in the ovary during the menstrual cycle are described below.

    1   Corpus luteum forms

    2   Ovulation occurs

    3   Progesterone is produced

    4   Corpus luteum degenerates

    5   Graafian follicle develops

    The sequence in which these changes occur following menstruation is

    A   2, 3, 1, 5, 4

    B   2, 1, 3, 4, 5

    C   5, 3, 2, 1, 4

    D   5, 2, 1, 3, 4.

11. Which of the following changes indicate ovulation is likely to have taken place?

	Cervical mucus	Body temperature
A	becomes sticky	rises
B	becomes sticky	falls
C	becomes watery	rises
D	becomes watery	falls

12. Which of the following babies would be most likely to require a blood transfusion immediately after birth?

    A   The first baby of a Rhesus negative mother and Rhesus positive father

    B   The first baby of a Rhesus positive mother and Rhesus negative father

    C   The second baby of a Rhesus negative mother and Rhesus positive father

    D   The second baby of a Rhesus positive mother and Rhesus negative father

13. The diagram below shows the blood flow in the umbilical cord.

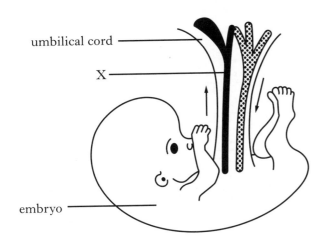

Which line in the table below identifies correctly blood vessel X and the blood it carries?

	Blood vessel X	Blood carried in X
A	vein	deoxygenated
B	vein	oxygenated
C	artery	deoxygenated
D	artery	oxygenated

14. Nicotine is a chemical which may affect pre-natal development.

The diagram shows the stages of development when major and minor malformations of organs may occur if there is exposure to nicotine.

Key ▬ major malformation
    ☐ minor malformation

	Stage of development (weeks after fertilisation)														
	Ball of cells		Embryo (organ formation)						Fetus (organ growth and development)						
	1	2	3	4	5	6	7	8	9	10	11	12	13	14	15
brain															
ear															
limbs															
genitalia															

For how many weeks during pregnancy is there a possibility of major malformations to organs during development?

A 6

B 7

C 9

D 13

15. Which of the following statements concerning the function of certain blood vessels is correct?

A   The vena cava carries oxygenated blood from the body to the right atrium.

B   The pulmonary artery carries deoxygenated blood to the lungs from the right ventricle.

C   The pulmonary vein carries oxygenated blood from the lungs to the left ventricle.

D   The aorta carries deoxygenated blood from the body to the left atrium.

[Turn over

16. Which line in the table below describes correctly the state of the heart valves during ventricular systole?

	Atrio-ventricular	Semi-lunar
A	open	open
B	closed	closed
C	open	closed
D	closed	open

17. The diagrams below represent two different body designs.

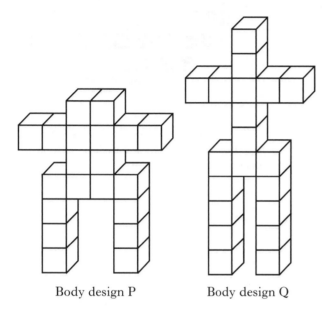

Body design P   Body design Q

Which of the following statements relating to these representations is correct?

A   Body P has the same volume as body Q.

B   Body P has a larger volume than body Q.

C   Body P has a larger surface area than body Q.

D   Body P has a larger surface area to volume ratio than body Q.

18. The graph below shows the effect of the carbon dioxide concentration of inhaled air on the breathing rate of an individual.

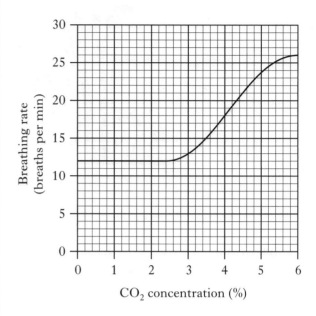

If the volume of one breath is 0·5 litre, what volume of air will be breathed in one minute when the CO_2 concentration is 4%?

A   6 litres

B   9 litres

C   18 litres

D   36 litres

19. The table below shows the changes in brain volume that have occurred during human evolution.

Time (million years ago)	Brain volume (cm³)
3	500
2	600
1	800
0	1400

By how much has brain volume increased during the last three million years?

A   36%

B   64%

C   180%

D   280%

20. Which sequence shows the correct order of the early stages of human infant motor development?

   A   Lifts head → rolls over → sits unsupported

   B   Sits unsupported → lifts head → rolls over

   C   Lifts head → sits unsupported → rolls over

   D   Rolls over → sits unsupported → lifts head

21. Vision in dim light is improved by the rods connecting to

   A   diverging neural pathways

   B   converging neural pathways

   C   reflex neural pathways

   D   peripheral neural pathways.

22. The serial position effect shows that words in the middle of a list are usually poorly recalled because many of these words

   A   have been displaced from short-term memory

   B   have not been encoded into short-term memory

   C   have been transferred into long-term memory

   D   have been stored in long-term memory.

23. The following factors influence development of phenotype.

   1   Environmental factors

   2   Genetic factors

   3   Maturation factors

   In the study of monozygotic twins, which of these factors can be discounted?

   A   1 only

   B   2 only

   C   1 and 2 only

   D   1, 2 and 3

24. The following histogram shows the percentage distribution of IQ rating in a sample of 1000 Scottish children.

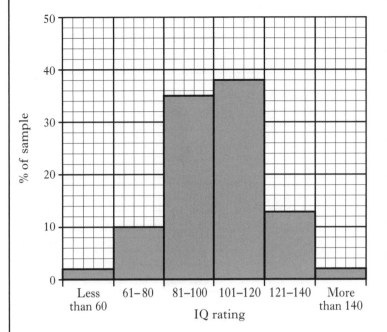

How many children have an IQ of over 100?

   A   38

   B   53

   C   380

   D   530

25. Four groups of students were asked to make paper aeroplanes.

   Each student had to make five aeroplanes.

   The table below shows the conditions under which each group worked.

	Demonstration on how to fold the paper	Written set of instructions supplied	Prize for the first student finished
Group 1	no	yes	no
Group 2	yes	no	no
Group 3	yes	no	yes
Group 4	yes	yes	yes

   Which two groups are likely to be affected by social facilitation?

   A   Groups 1 and 4

   B   Groups 2 and 3

   C   Groups 2 and 4

   D   Groups 3 and 4

26. The figures below show the population structure of a developed and a developing country.

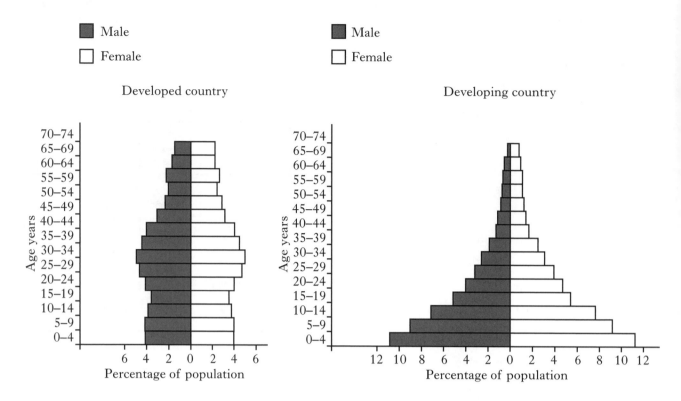

The percentage of the population under ten years of age in the developing country exceeds that of the developed country by

A   12%

B   14%

C   24%

D   32%.

27. The diagram below shows the relative movement of carbon within the carbon cycle.
(*Units are kg × 10^{12} carbon per year*)

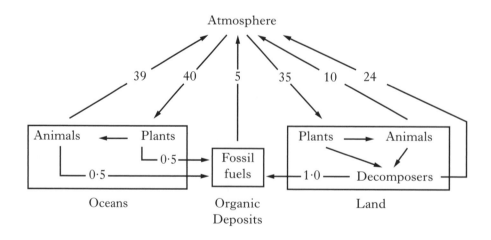

Which component of the carbon cycle shows a net loss of carbon?

A   Atmosphere

B   Oceans

C   Land

D   Organic deposits

28. The apparatus shown below was used to investigate the effect of concentration of phosphate on the growth of grass seedlings.

Grass seedlings were grown in seven different culture solutions.

The height of the grass seedlings was measured after 6 weeks.

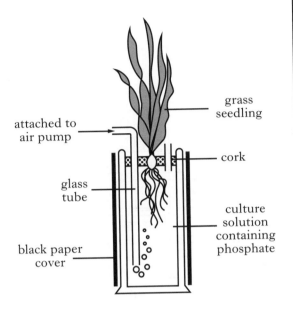

Two variables that must be the same throughout this investigation are

A   volume of culture solution and concentration of phosphate in the culture solution

B   concentration of phosphate in the culture solution and light intensity

C   light intensity and temperature

D   temperature and the height of the grass seedlings.

29. The diagram below shows a simplified outline of the nitrogen cycle.

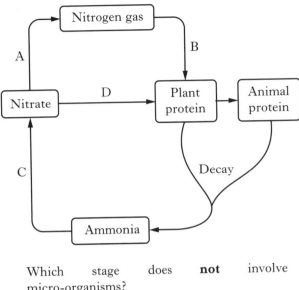

Which stage does **not** involve micro-organisms?

30. Apple crop yields have been increased by plant breeders selecting for

A   disease resistance

B   flavour

C   resistance to bruising

D   sugar content.

Candidates are reminded that the answer sheet MUST be returned INSIDE the front cover of this answer booklet.

[Turn over for Section B on *page ten*

DO N
WRI
IN T
MAR

SECTION B

Marks

All questions in this section should be attempted.

All answers must be written clearly and legibly in ink.

1. Trypsin is an enzyme which catalyses the breakdown of proteins in the small intestine.

   The graphs below show how pH and temperature affect the activity of trypsin.

   Graph 1—effect of pH on trypsin activity

   Graph 2—effect of temperature on trypsin activity

   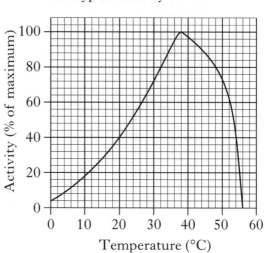

   (*a*) (i) State the optimum conditions for trypsin activity.

   pH _____   temperature _____ °C   **1**

   (ii) State the range of conditions over which trypsin shows at least 40% of its maximum activity.

   _____

   _____   **1**

   (iii) Explain the rapid decrease in activity shown in Graph 2.

   _____

   _____

   _____   **2**

DO NOT WRITE IN THIS MARGIN

Marks

1. (continued)

(*b*) The pancreas produces and releases trypsinogen which does not breakdown proteins. In the lumen of the small intestine, trypsinogen is converted to trypsin by the enzyme enterokinase.

$$\text{trypsinogen} \xrightarrow{\textit{enterokinase}} \text{trypsin}$$

(i) What term describes the effect of enterokinase in this reaction?

______________________________ **1**

(ii) Explain why trypsinogen is produced in the pancreas instead of trypsin.

____

____ **1**

[Turn over

Marks

2. The diagram below shows the metabolism of three energy sources in a cell.

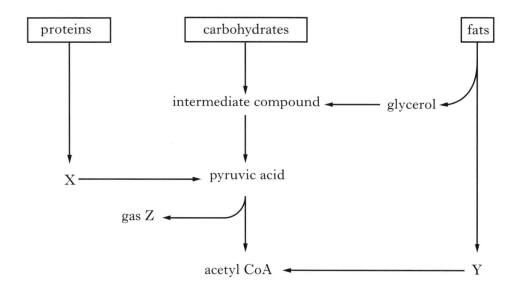

(a) Name X, Y and Z.

X _____

Y _____

Z _____   **2**

(b) What term describes the breakdown of carbohydrate into pyruvic acid during respiration?

_____   **1**

(c) Describe what happens to acetyl CoA after it enters the Krebs Cycle.

_____

_____   **1**

(d) Under what circumstances would the body gain most of its energy from proteins?

_____   **1**

(e) Carbohydrate is stored in the body as a polysaccharide.

Name this polysaccharide and state where it is stored.

Name _____

Storage location _____   **1**

3. The diagram below shows the structure of one strain of the influenza virus.

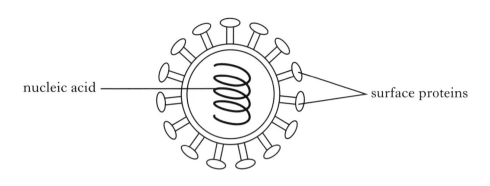

nucleic acid —————— surface proteins

(a) This virus can be used to prepare a flu vaccine. In order to do this the nucleic acid must be broken up but the surface proteins left intact.

Explain why it is necessary to:

(i) break up the nucleic acid _____

_____

(ii) leave the surface proteins intact _____

_____ **2**

(b) After a flu epidemic, two individuals, X and Y, were found to possess antibodies against this strain of influenza. X had recently recovered from flu while Y had been given a vaccine against it.

Complete the following sentences by <u>underlining</u> one option from each pair shown in **bold**.

The immunity gained by X is **active/passive** and **naturally/artificially** acquired.

The immunity gained by Y is **active/passive** and **naturally/artificially** acquired. **2**

(c) A different vaccine is required against each strain of the influenza virus.

Suggest why different vaccines are required.

_____

_____ **1**

(d) Researchers are attempting to develop a new vaccine which will be effective against **all** strains of the influenza virus. Trials of this new vaccine have shown that it increases the activity of T-lymphocytes in the body.

Describe the method by which T-lymphocytes combat infection.

_____

_____ **1**

Marks

[Turn over

Marks

4. Haemophilia is a sex-linked disorder caused by a recessive allele (h) which results in an individual producing a faulty blood-clotting protein.

The diagram below shows the sex chromosomes from two individuals.

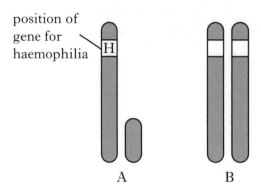

(*a*) Individual A is male while individual B is a female carrier of the allele for haemophilia.

   (i) **Complete the diagram** by labelling the alleles on the sex chromosomes of individual B.   **1**

   (ii) State the genotypes of individuals A and B.

   A _____   B _____   **1**

   (iii) What is the chance that a daughter produced by this couple will have haemophilia?

   Explain your answer.

   Space for calculation

   Chance_____%

   Explanation_____

   _____   **1**

(*b*) Karyotypes are images of fetal chromosomes arranged in homologous pairs.

   (i) State **one** feature of chromosomes which allows them to be paired in this way.

   _____   **1**

   (ii) A mutation can occur during meiosis, in which chromosomes fail to separate. This results in an extra chromosome appearing in the karyotype.

   What term is used to describe the failure of chromosomes to separate during meiosis?

   _____   **1**

Marks

5. The flowchart summarises the processes involved in the production of semen.

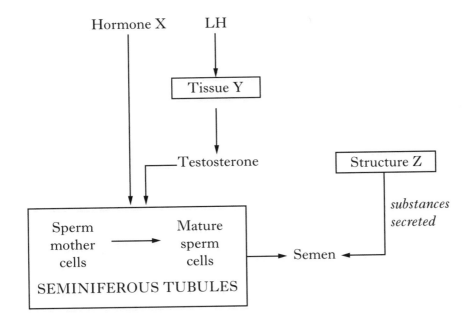

(a) Name hormone X and tissue Y.

Hormone X_____

Tissue Y_____   2

(b) Semen contains substances secreted by structure Z.

(i) Identify structure Z.

_____   1

(ii) Describe how a named substance from structure Z aids fertilisation.

Substance_____

Description _____

_____   1

(c) Complete the table to show the percentage of each type of cell which would contain a Y chromosome.

Cells	Percentage of cells containing a Y chromosome
Sperm mother cells	
Mature sperm cells	

1

[Turn over

6. The graphs below show changes in the volume and composition of milk produced by a woman in the first week following the birth of her child.

Graph 1—changes in the volume of milk produced

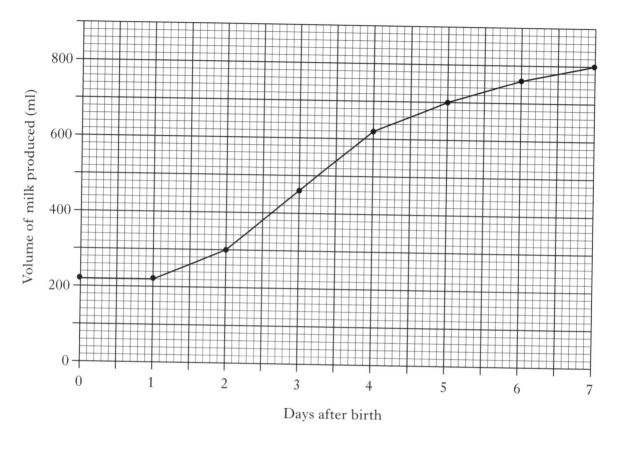

Graph 2—changes in the concentration of lactose sugar and IgA antibody in milk

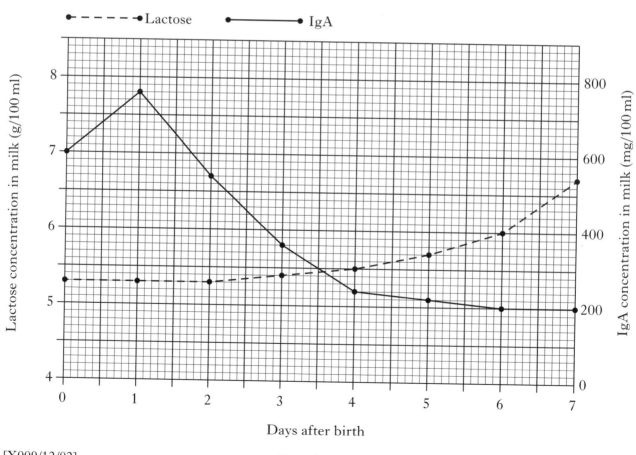

Marks

6. **(continued)**

(*a*)   (i)   What name is given to milk produced in the first few days after birth?

_____   1

   (ii)   From **Graph 2**, describe **two** ways in which the composition of milk produced in the first three days after birth differs from milk produced later.

   1_____

   2_____   1

(*b*)   What was the volume of milk produced on day 3?

_____   1

(*c*)   (i)   Between days 2 and 3 this woman produced a constant mass of IgA.

   Explain why the concentration of IgA in her milk decreased during this time.

   _____

   _____   1

   (ii)   Express, as a simple whole number ratio, the concentration of IgA compared to the concentration of lactose produced on day 6.

   (1 g = 1000 mg)

   Space for calculation

_____ : _____   1
   IgA   Lactose

(*d*)   Using **Graphs 1** and **2**, calculate the mass of lactose produced on day 5.

   Space for calculation

_____ g   1

[Turn over

Marks

7. The diagram below shows some blood vessels within muscle tissue of an athlete. The direction of blood flow is indicated by the arrows.

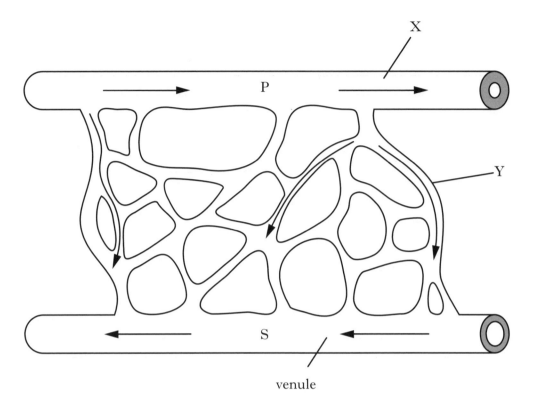

venule

(a) Name the type of blood vessels labelled X and Y.

X _____

Y _____   1

(b) Name **two** substances which are at a higher concentration in the blood at point P than at point S.

1 _____

2 _____   1

(c) The athlete ran on a treadmill at high speed for ten minutes.

Explain why the concentration of lactic acid in his blood increased during this time.

_____

_____   1

(d) Tissue fluid surrounds the muscle cells.

Some of this fluid is reabsorbed into the bloodstream.

How else is tissue fluid removed from around the muscle cells?

_____   1

Marks

8. The graph below shows changes in the volume of blood in the left ventricle of a man's heart.

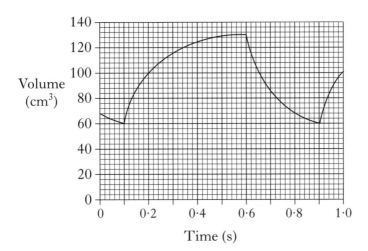

(a) How long does ventricular systole last?

_____ s   **1**

(b) (i) What is the heart rate of this man?

_____ beats per minute   **1**

    (ii) Calculate the volume of blood leaving this man's left ventricle every minute.

Space for calculation

_____ cm³   **1**

(c) When this man exercises, the volume of blood leaving his heart increases significantly.

Describe how the nervous system and hormones cause this increase.

_____

_____

_____

_____

_____

_____   **3**

Marks

9. Infants and elderly people are especially vulnerable to hypothermia.

(*a*) (i) What is hypothermia?

_____

_____   **1**

(ii) State a **biological reason** why elderly people are particularly vulnerable to hypothermia.

_____

_____   **1**

(iii) Explain why an infant's small body size makes him more vulnerable to hypothermia than a teenager.

_____

_____   **1**

(*b*) (i) Name the body's temperature monitoring centre.

_____   **1**

(ii) Explain how the following cause a decrease in body temperature.

1 Increased sweating _____

_____

2 Vasodilation _____

_____   **2**

Marks

10. The diagram below shows a neurone from an adult.

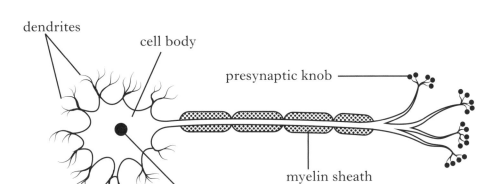

(a) Draw an arrow **on the diagram** to show the direction in which an impulse would travel.   1

(b) Suggest a possible role of the nucleus in the transfer of information across a synapse.

_____

_____   1

(c) Complete the table below which contains information about organelles found in the presynaptic knob.

Organelle	*Function*
	Provides ATP for synthesis reactions
Vesicle	

1

(d) (i) How might a neurone in a newly-born child differ from the one in the diagram?

_____   1

(ii) In what way would this affect how the neurone functions?

_____

_____   1

[Turn over

DO N
WRI
IN T
MAR

Marks

11. Split brain patients cannot transfer information between their left and right cerebral hemispheres because the band of nerve fibres connecting these areas of the brain has been cut.

(a) Name the band of fibres which connects the two hemispheres.

_____

1

(b) Some of the functions of each hemisphere are described in the table below. These functions are unaffected in split brain patients.

Left cerebral hemisphere	Right cerebral hemisphere
processes information from right eye	processes information from left eye
controls language production	controls movements of left hand

The diagram below shows an experiment on a split brain patient.

The patient was asked to stare at a spot in the centre of a screen and the words "key" and "spoon" were flashed briefly onto the screen in the positions shown.

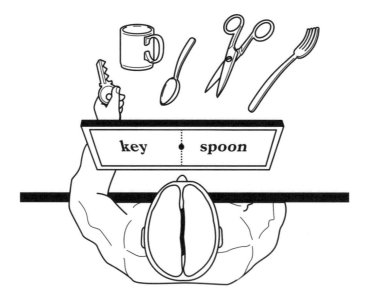

(i) The patient was then told to use his left hand to pick up the objects he saw named on the screen.

Explain why the patient picked up the key but not the spoon.

_____

_____

_____

_____

2

DO NOT WRITE IN THIS MARGIN

Marks

11. (continued)

(ii) The patient was then asked to say what he saw written on the screen.

Predict what he would have said and give a reason for your answer.

Prediction ______________ **1**

Reason ______________________________

____

______________________________ **1**

[Turn over

Marks

12. The following question relates to aspects of learning associated with guitar playing.

(a) What effect does practising a motor skill, such as repeatedly playing chords, have on the nervous system?

_____

_____ 1

(b) Suggest how "shaping" might be used by a teacher to help students improve their guitar playing over the course of a year.

_____

_____

_____

_____ 2

(c) (i) A teenager decides that she dislikes all of a band's music after hearing just one song.

What form of learning is this?

_____ 1

(ii) As she grows older this teenager's opinion about the band's music could be altered by internalisation.

Explain how this may happen.

_____

_____ 1

DO NOT WRITE IN THIS MARGIN

Marks

12. (continued)

(*d*) Anti-social behaviour can occur when people are together in a group such as at a music festival.

What is the name of this effect and why does it occur?

Name ______________________________ **1**

Cause ____

____ **1**

[Turn over

Marks

13. The diagram shows land use within a valley in a developing country.

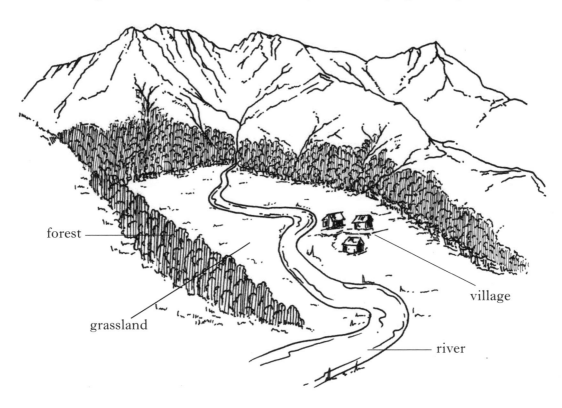

forest

grassland

village

river

(a) The population of the village near the river is increasing and the village is expanding.

(i) State **one** way in which the land around the village would change if this expansion continued.

Explain why this change would occur.

Change_____

Explanation_____

_____   1

(ii) How might the resulting increase in the human population affect the river?

_____

_____   1

DO NOT
WRITE
IN THIS
MARGIN

Marks

13. (continued)

(b) Some changes in land use increase methane release into the atmosphere.

Give an example of such a change and state how methane release affects planet Earth.

Example _____

Effect _____   1

(c) What name is given to the study of changes in the size of human populations?

_____   1

[Turn over

Marks

14. An investigation was carried out to find out where pollution was entering a loch. A student suspected that chemicals were entering the loch through one of the rivers that flowed into it (Figure 1).

   She collected a water sample from each of the three rivers that entered the loch. She then measured the concentration of nitrates and phosphates present in each sample. Her results are shown in the table below.

Figure 1—map showing loch and rivers that enter it.   **Table**—analysis of water samples

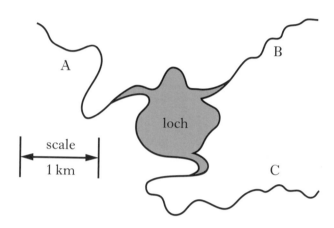

	Concentration of chemicals in water (mg/l)	
River	Nitrate	Phosphate
A	2	0
B	35	10
C	5	1

   (a) Construct a bar graph to show the data in the table.

   (Additional graph paper, if required, can be found on *Page thirty-four*.)

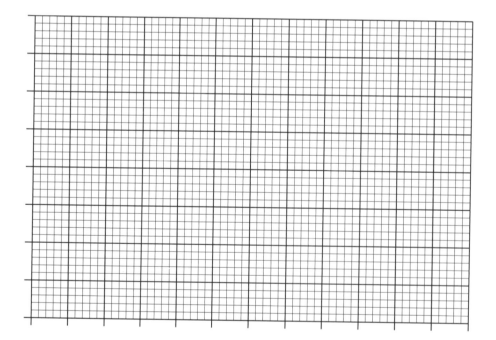

3

Marks

14. (continued)

(b) What conclusion can be drawn from the results of this investigation?

_____

_____   1

(c) State **two** variables which would have to be kept constant when collecting the water samples from each river.

1 _____

2 _____   1

(d) How could the student improve the reliability of her results?

_____

_____   1

(e) Suggest how the student could extend her investigation to allow her to locate more accurately the source of the polluting chemicals.

_____

_____   1

(f) The results of this investigation were obtained in the summer.

Suggest why there would be a lower concentration of nitrates in all of the rivers if the investigation had been carried out in the winter.

_____

_____   1

(g) Describe the effects of excess nitrates entering a loch in summer.

_____

_____

_____   1

[Turn over for Section C on *Page thirty*

DO N
WRI
IN T
MAR

SECTION C

Marks

Both questions in this section should be attempted.

Note that each question contains a choice.

Questions 1 and 2 should be attempted on the blank pages which follow.

Supplementary sheets, if required, may be obtained from the Invigilator.

Labelled diagrams may be used where appropriate.

1. Answer **either** A **or** B.

    A   Give an account of transport across the cell membrane under the following headings:

    (i)   the structure of the membrane;   3

    (ii)   osmotic effects on cells;   2

    (iii) endocytosis and exocytosis.   5

                                                                (10)

    OR

    B   Give an account of the process of meiosis under the following headings:

    (i)   first meiotic division;   6

    (ii)   second meiotic division;   2

    (iii) significance of the process.   2

                                                                (10)

In question 2, ONE mark is available for coherence and ONE mark is available for relevance.

2. Answer **either** A **or** B.

    A   Describe processes that occur in the liver which bring about changes in the composition of the blood.   **(10)**

    OR

    B   Describe processes that occur in the kidney which bring about changes in the composition of the blood.   **(10)**

[END OF QUESTION PAPER]

DO NOT
WRITE
IN THIS
MARGIN

SPACE FOR ANSWERS

SPACE FOR ANSWERS

SPACE FOR ANSWERS

SPACE FOR ANSWERS

ADDITIONAL GRAPH FOR QUESTION 14(*a*)

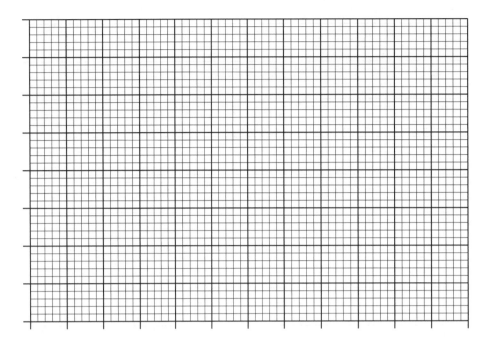

HIGHER

2014

HODDER
GIBSON
LEARN MORE

[BLANK PAGE]

FOR OFFICIAL USE

Total for
Sections B & C

X009/12/02

NATIONAL
QUALIFICATIONS
2014

FRIDAY, 16 MAY
1.00 PM – 3.30 PM

HUMAN BIOLOGY
HIGHER

Fill in these boxes and read what is printed below.

Full name of centre

Town

Forename(s)

Surname

Date of birth

Day   Month   Year   Scottish candidate number   Number of seat

SECTION A—Questions 1–30 (30 marks)

Instructions for completion of Section A are given on page two.

For this section of the examination you must use an **HB pencil**.

SECTIONS B AND C (100 marks)

1 (a)   All questions should be attempted.

   (b)   It should be noted that in **Section C** questions 1 and 2 each contain a choice.

2 The questions may be answered in any order but all answers are to be written in the spaces provided in this answer book, **and must be written clearly and legibly in ink**.

3 Additional space for answers will be found at the end of the book. If further space is required, supplementary sheets may be obtained from the Invigilator and should be inserted inside the **front** cover of this book.

4 The numbers of questions must be clearly inserted with any answers written in the additional space.

5 Rough work, if any should be necessary, should be written in this book and then scored through when the fair copy has been written. If further space is required a supplementary sheet for rough work may be obtained from the Invigilator.

6 Before leaving the examination room you must give this book to the Invigilator. If you do not, you may lose all the marks for this paper.

Read carefully

1   Check that the answer sheet provided is for **Human Biology Higher (Section A)**.

2   For this section of the examination you must use an **HB pencil**, and where necessary, an eraser.

3   Check that the answer sheet you have been given has **your name**, **date of birth**, **SCN** (Scottish Candidate Number) and **Centre Name** printed on it.

Do not change any of these details.

4   If any of this information is wrong, tell the Invigilator immediately.

5   If this information is correct, **print** your name and seat number in the boxes provided.

6   The answer to each question is **either** A, B, C or D. Decide what your answer is, then, using your pencil, put a horizontal line in the space provided (see sample question below).

7   There is **only one correct** answer to each question.

8   Any rough working should be done on the question paper or the rough working sheet, not on your answer sheet.

9   At the end of the examination, put the **answer sheet for Section A inside the front cover of this answer book**.

Sample Question

The digestive enzyme pepsin is most active in the

A   stomach

B   mouth

C   duodenum

D   pancreas.

The correct answer is **A**—stomach. The answer **A** has been clearly marked in **pencil** with a horizontal line (see below).

A   B   C   D

Changing an answer

If you decide to change your answer, carefully erase your first answer and, using your pencil, fill in the answer you want. The answer below has been changed to **D**.

A   B   C   D

SECTION A

All questions in this section should be attempted.

Answers should be given on the separate answer sheet provided.

1. Non-competitive inhibitors affect enzyme action by

   A   altering the shape of the active site of the enzyme

   B   altering the shape of the substrate molecule

   C   competing for the active site of the enzyme

   D   acting as a co-enzyme for enzyme action.

2. The diagram below shows the activation of three inactive enzymes released into the small intestine by the pancreas.

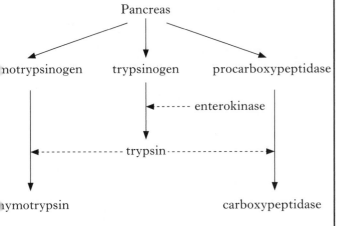

How many enzyme activators are shown in this diagram?

   A   4

   B   3

   C   2

   D   1

3. Which of the following substances contains nitrogen?

   A   Glucagon

   B   Glucose

   C   Glycerol

   D   Glycogen

4. The following diagram illustrates the fluid mosaic model of a cell membrane.

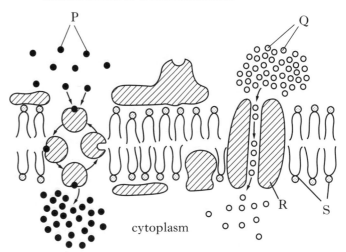

Which line in the table below describes correctly the uptake of substances P and Q and the nature of substances R and S?

	Uptake of substance		Nature of substance	
	P	Q	R	S
A	passive	active	protein	phospholipid
B	active	passive	phospholipid	protein
C	passive	active	phospholipid	protein
D	active	passive	protein	phospholipid

5. The diagram below represents part of the plasma membrane of a red blood cell.

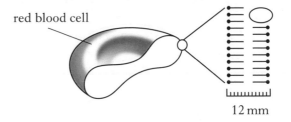

The membrane is shown magnified 2 million times.

What is the width of the membrane?
(1 nanometre $= 1 \times 10^{-6}$ mm)

   A   0·6 nanometres

   B   6 nanometres

   C   24 nanometres

   D   60 nanometres

6. A person with blood group AB can safely receive blood from

    A   any blood group

    B   blood group O only

    C   blood groups A and B only

    D   blood group AB only.

7. Which substances must be provided by host cells for the synthesis of viruses?

    A   Proteins and nucleotides

    B   Amino acids and DNA

    C   Proteins and DNA

    D   Amino acids and nucleotides

8. A DNA molecule replicates three times during three cell division processes.

    How many of the 8 resulting DNA molecules will contain the original DNA strands?

    A   0

    B   2

    C   4

    D   8

9. Which of the following are produced by meiosis?

    A   Haploid cells of identical genetic composition

    B   Diploid cells of different genetic composition

    C   Diploid cells of identical genetic composition

    D   Haploid cells of different genetic composition

10. The chromosomes of a gamete mother cell are shown in the diagram below.

    How many chromosomes would be present in each gamete formed?

    A   2

    B   4

    C   8

    D   16

11. Huntington's chorea is caused by a single dominant gene which is not sex-linked.

    A woman's father is heterozygous for this condition and her mother is unaffected.

    What are the chances that this woman has inherited the condition?

    A   75%

    B   67%

    C   50%

    D   25%

12. Which of the following is **not** a function of the secretions from the prostate gland and seminal vesicles?

    A   They add sperm to semen

    B   They add sugar to semen

    C   They add fluid to semen

    D   They add enzymes to semen

13. How many days after ovulation is menstruation most likely to occur?

    A   5

    B   10

    C   15

    D   20

14. Which fertility treatment would be appropriate for a woman with blocked uterine tubes?

A   Calculation of fertile period

B   Provision of fertility drugs

C   Artificial insemination

D   *In vitro* fertilisation

15. Which of the following processes describes how antibodies are exchanged between the maternal and fetal circulations?

A   Active transport

B   Pinocytosis

C   Osmosis

D   Diffusion

16. Which line in the table below identifies correctly conditions which would increase the risk of the fetus being harmed by the mother's immune system?

	Pregnancy	Blood type of Mother	Blood type of Fetus
A	First	Rhesus negative	Rhesus positive
B	Second	Rhesus positive	Rhesus negative
C	First	Rhesus positive	Rhesus negative
D	Second	Rhesus negative	Rhesus positive

17. The graphs below show the average yearly increase in height of girls and boys.

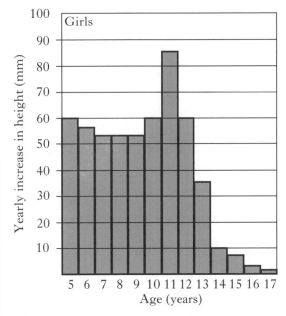

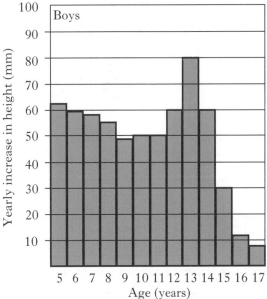

Which of the following statements is correct?

A   The greatest yearly increase for boys occurs one year later than the greatest yearly increase for girls.

B   Boys are still growing at seventeen but girls have stopped growing by this age.

C   Between the ages of five and eight boys grow more than girls.

D   There is no age when boys and girls show the same average yearly increase in height.

[Turn over

18. The main blood vessel supplying the heart muscle itself with oxygenated blood is the

A   coronary vein

B   coronary artery

C   pulmonary artery

D   pulmonary vein.

19. The diagram below shows a section through the human heart.

Where is the sinoartrial node (SAN) located?

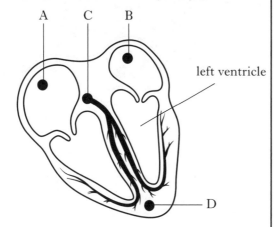

20. The graph below shows the effect of training and age on oxygen uptake.

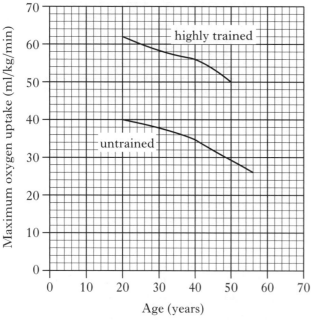

What is the percentage increase in maximum oxygen uptake for a 20-year-old untrained person who becomes highly trained?

A   22·0%

B   55·0%

C   62·0%

D   64·5%

21. Which line in the table below identifies correctly the effect of increased secretion of anti-diuretic hormone (ADH) on the composition and volume of urine?

	Concentration of urea	Concentration of glucose	Volume of urine
A	no change	no change	increase
B	increase	increase	decrease
C	increase	no change	decrease
D	decrease	no change	increase

22. An experiment was carried out to estimate the concentration of urea present in urine samples.

The method involved adding tablets of the enzyme urease to the urine samples in a boiling tube and timing how long it takes for the litmus paper to turn blue.

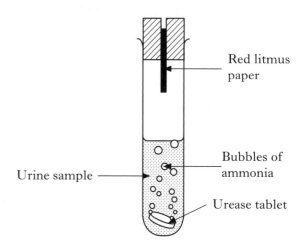

Which two factors would have to be kept the same throughout the investigation?

A   Size of tablet and concentration of urea

B   Concentration of urea and time

C   Size of tablet and volume of urine

D   Volume of urine and time

23. Which line in the table below describes correctly the control of body temperature?

	Monitoring centre	Form of communication	Regulating organ
A	skin	hormonal	liver
B	skin	nervous	brain
C	hypothalamus	hormonal	liver
D	hypothalamus	nervous	skin

24. Which parts of the body are controlled by the largest motor area of the cerebrum?

A   Hands and lips

B   Feet and hands

C   Ears and nose

D   Legs and arms

25. The following diagram represents four neurones in a nervous pathway.

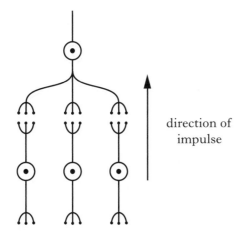

direction of impulse

Which line in the table below describes the pathway correctly?

	Type of pathway	
A	motor	divergent
B	motor	convergent
C	sensory	divergent
D	sensory	convergent

26. Students were asked to recall twelve letters of the alphabet in any order, after hearing the list of letters read out slowly. An analysis of their performance is shown in the graph below.

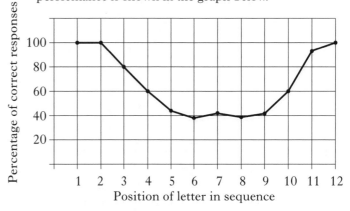

On how many occasions was a letter recalled by more than 50% of the students?

A   4

B   5

C   6

D   7

27. The table below shows the average yield in the years 1890 and 1990 for four crops grown in Scotland.

	Crop	Average yield (tonnes per hectare)	
		1890	1990
A	Barley	2·4	6·6
B	Wheat	2·7	8·1
C	Turnip	4·5	10·0
D	Potato	15·0	37·5

Which crop has shown the greatest percentage increase in average yield?

[Turn over

28. The graph below shows the number of cases of meningitis and deaths due to meningitis in the UK from 1998 to 2001.

KEY	
□	cases
—•—	deaths

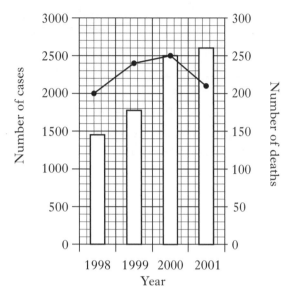

In which year was the number of deaths from meningitis less than 10% of the number of cases?

A   1998

B   1999

C   2000

D   2001

29. An algal bloom in a loch may result from

A   lack of oxygen

B   lack of sunlight

C   excess phosphates

D   excess herbicide.

30. The map below represents a short length of a Scottish river.

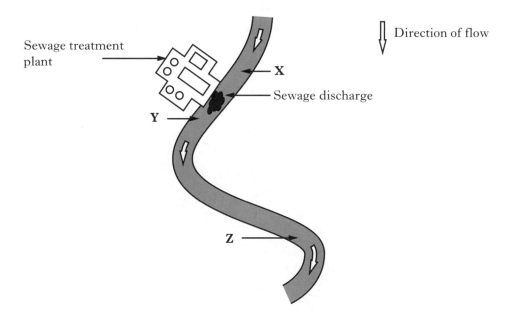

There was an accidental discharge of untreated sewage into the river.

Which line in the table below shows the likely changes in the population of bacteria between points **X** and **Y**, and between points **Y** and **Z**?

	Change in the bacterial population	
	Between points **X** *and* **Y**	*Between points* **Y** *and* **Z**
A	increase	no change
B	increase	decrease
C	decrease	no change
D	decrease	decrease

Candidates are reminded that the answer sheet MUST be returned INSIDE the front cover of this answer booklet.

[Turn over for Section B on *page ten*

SECTION B   *Marks*

All questions in this section should be attempted.

All answers must be written clearly and legibly in ink.

1. The diagram below shows some skeletal muscle cells.

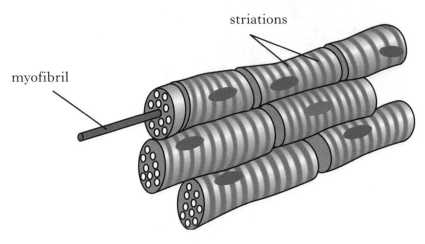

(a) Name the **two** proteins that give rise to the striations in the muscle cells.

    1 ——————————— 2 ———————————————   **1**

(b) The arrangement of the protein filaments in the muscle is shown in the two diagrams below.

    Diagram A represents the arrangement of the filaments in the labelled myofibril.

    Diagram B represents a cross section through this myofibril.

    Diagram A   **Diagram B**

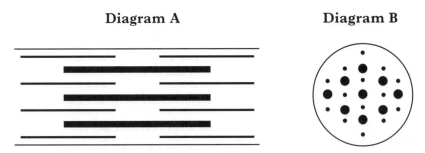

    (i) **Draw a line on Diagram A** to show where the cross section was taken.   **1**

    (ii) Describe what happens to the arrangement of protein filaments when the muscle contracts.

    ————————————————————————————————————

    ————————————————————————————————————   **1**

DO NOT WRITE IN THIS MARGIN

Marks

1. (continued)

(*c*) Respiration produces the ATP required for muscle contraction.

Explain why only small amounts of ATP are produced during anaerobic respiration.

____

____

____

____ **2**

[Turn over

Marks

2. Yeast is a single-celled fungus which produces enzymes, one of which catalyses the release of hydrogen during respiration.

An investigation was carried out to compare three sugars as respiratory substrates for yeast. Methylene blue dye was used to measure the rate of respiration because it turns clear in the presence of hydrogen.

A colorimeter was used to measure the colour intensity of the dye during the investigation.

The investigation setup is shown in **Figure 1**.

Table 1 shows the range of colorimeter readings recorded.

Figure 1

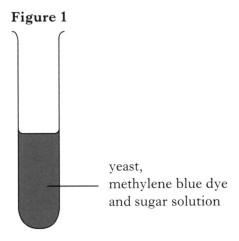

yeast,
methylene blue dye
and sugar solution

Table 1

Colour intensity of dye	Colorimeter reading (units)
maximum	63
minimum	0

Three test tubes were set up, each containing a different sugar. The colour intensity of the dye was measured at four-minute intervals for twenty minutes.

The results of the investigation are shown in **Table 2** below.

Table 2

Time (min)	Colorimeter reading (units)		
	glucose sugar	maltose sugar	lactose sugar
0	63	63	63
4	46	61	63
8	28	56	63
12	10	35	63
16	0	10	63
20	0	0	63

(a) When setting up the test tubes as shown in **Figure 1**, state which substance should be added last.

Give a reason for your choice of substance.

Substance _____

Reason _____

_____

1

Marks

2. **(continued)**

(b) List **three** variables which would have to be kept constant during this investigation.

1 _____

2 _____

3 _____   **2**

(c) State how the reliability of the results from this investigation could be improved.

_____

_____   **1**

(d)   (i)   Construct a line graph to show all the data in **Table 2**.

(Additional graph paper, if required, can be found on *Page thirty-five*.)

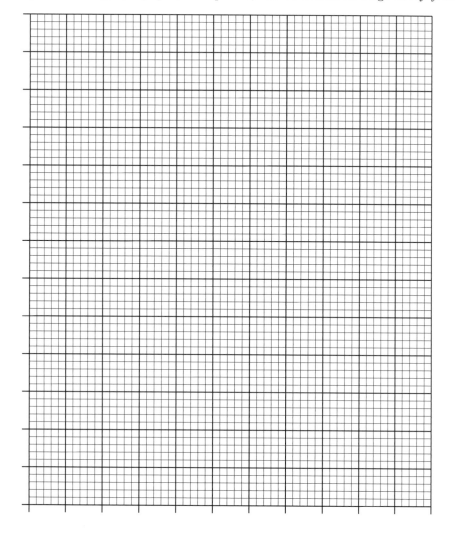

3

(ii)   State a conclusion that can be drawn from the results of this investigation.

_____

_____   **1**

Marks

2. **(continued)**

(e) (i) Maltose is a disaccharide sugar which is composed of two glucose molecules joined together.

Use this information to explain why the colour intensity of the dye in the test tube containing maltose decreased more slowly than the intensity of the dye in the test tube containing glucose.

_____

_____ 1

(ii) Lactose is also a disaccharide sugar.

Suggest why the colour intensity of the dye in the test tube containing lactose remained the same throughout the investigation.

_____

_____ 1

Marks

3. The diagram below illustrates the stages involved in the destruction of a bacterial cell by phagocytosis.

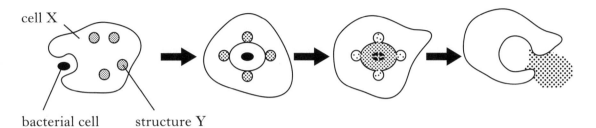

cell X

bacterial cell   structure Y

Stage: **A**   **B**   **C**   **D**

(a)   (i)   Name the type of phagocytic cell labelled X.

_____   1

(ii)   Name structure Y and describe its function during stages B and C.

Structure Y _____

Function _____

_____

_____

_____   2

(iii) What term describes the secretory process shown in stage D?

_____   1

(b)   Bacteria entering the body may also trigger the humoral response.

Describe what happens during the humoral response.

_____

_____

_____

_____   2

[Turn over

Marks

4. The diagram below shows the inheritance of a sex-linked condition in a family.

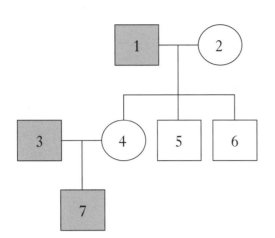

	= unaffected female
	= affected female
	= unaffected male
	= affected male

(a) The condition is caused by a recessive sex-linked allele represented by the letter **d**.

   (i) State the genotypes of individuals 3 and 4.

   Individual 3 _____

   Individual 4 _____   1

   (ii) Explain why individual 1 could not pass the condition to his sons.

   _____

   _____

   _____   1

   (iii) Individual 6 has a son with a woman who is a carrier of the condition.
   Calculate the percentage chance of their son having this condition.
   Space for calculation

   _____ %   1

DO NOT WRITE IN THIS MARGIN

Marks

4. (continued)

(*b*) The condition is caused by a mutation in which an extra nucleotide is inserted into the gene that codes for an enzyme.

Explain the likely effect of this mutation on the structure of the enzyme.

____

____

____

____ **2**

(*c*) The condition occurs with a frequency of 1 in 350 males.

Assuming an equal proportion of males and females, calculate how many males are likely to have the condition in a town with a population of 175 000.

Space for calculation

____________ **1**

[Turn over

Marks

5. The diagram below shows the fertilisation of an ovum and its subsequent early development.

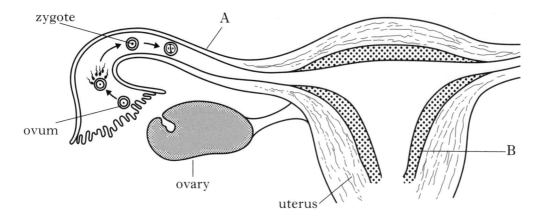

(a) Name structures A and B.

A _____

B _____   2

(b) The ovum is released from the Graafian follicle which then becomes the corpus luteum. These structures are affected by pituitary hormones.

Complete the table below to describe the effect of these hormones on the structures.

Structure	Pituitary hormone	Effect on structure
Graafian follicle	FSH	
Corpus luteum	LH	

2

(c) During its journey down structure A, the zygote undergoes repeated cell divisions.

What name is given to this series of early cell divisions?

_____   1

(d) The further development of the zygote shown resulted in the birth of monozygotic twins.

Describe how this occurred.

_____

_____   1

Marks

6. The diagram below shows an electrocardiogram (ECG) trace of an individual's heartbeat.

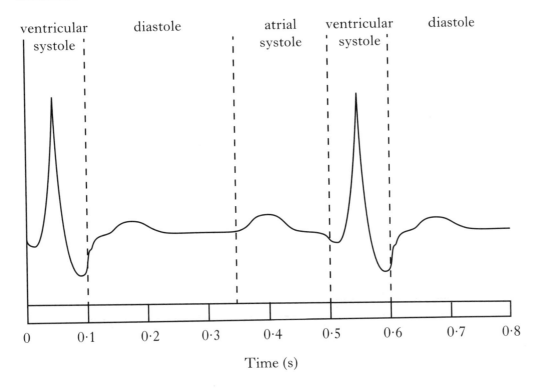

Time (s)

(a) Calculate the heart rate of this individual.

Space for calculation

_____ bpm   **1**

(b) Complete the following sentence by underlining one option from each pair of options shown in **bold**.

During the diastole stage of the cardiac cycle, the atrial muscles are **contracted / relaxed** and the ventricular muscles are **contracted / relaxed**.   **1**

(c) Name the valves which will be open and closed in the left side of the heart during ventricular systole.

Open _____ Closed _____   **1**

(d) Predict how this individual's ECG trace would change under the influence of the parasympathetic nervous system.

_____

_____   **1**

[Turn over

Marks

7. The graph below shows the changes in the concentration of glucose and insulin in a cyclist's blood while he cycled at a constant rate for two hours.

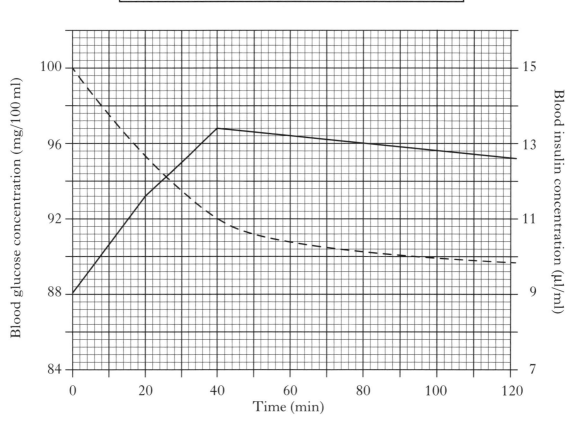

(a) (i) State the cyclist's blood insulin concentration after he had been cycling for 10 minutes.

_____   1

(ii) State the cyclist's blood glucose concentration when his blood insulin concentration was 11 µl/ml.

_____ mg/100 ml   1

(b) During exercise, adrenaline is released which inhibits the production of insulin.

Explain why this is important to the cyclist.

_____

_____

_____

_____   2

7. (continued)

Marks

(c) The graph below shows the changes that occurred in the distribution of blood to some parts of the cyclist's body after he had been cycling for 20 minutes.

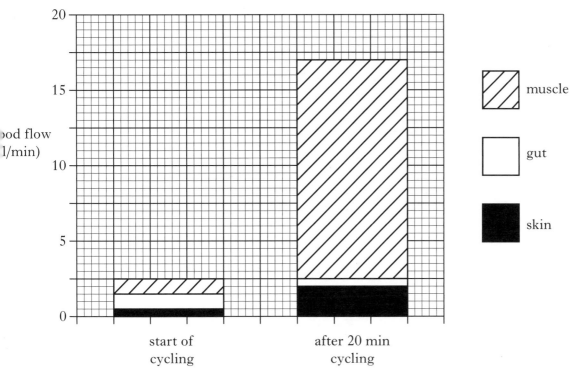

(i) Calculate the percentage increase that occurred in blood flow to his skin after he had been cycling for 20 minutes.

Space for calculation

_____ %   **1**

(ii) Calculate the whole number ratio of muscle to gut blood flow after 20 minutes of cycling.

Space for calculation

_____ : _____   **1**
 muscle   gut

(iii) Describe how changes in the volume and distribution of blood to the muscles occur during cycling.

Volume _____

_____

Distribution _____

_____   **2**

Marks

8. The diagram below shows the relationship between a blood capillary, body cells and a lymphatic vessel.

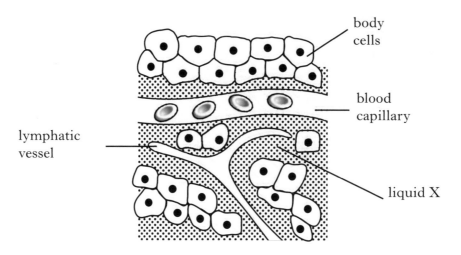

(*a*) (i) Name liquid X.

_____   1

(ii) State **one** way in which the composition of this liquid is different from blood plasma.

_____   1

(*b*) Complete the table below by naming **one** substance, apart from carbon dioxide and water, which is passed from the cells in each of the following tissues into blood capillaries.

Tissue	Substance
Interstitial cells	
Pancreas	
Leg muscle (after a sprint)	

2

(*c*) Explain how lymph is transported in lymphatic vessels.

_____

_____

_____   2

Marks

9. The diagram below shows blood vessels associated with the liver.

The arrows show the direction of blood flow in these vessels.

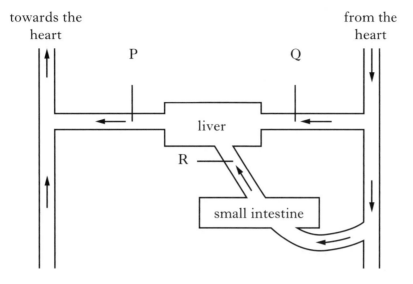

    towards the   from the
heart   heart

(*a*)   (i)   Identify the blood vessels labelled Q and R.

           Q _____

           R _____   2

    (ii) During the digestion of a meal, which of the three blood vessels would have the highest concentration of:

           1 Glucose _____

           2 Urea _____   1

(*b*)   The liver breaks down red blood cells.

    Describe what happens to the products of haemoglobin breakdown.

    _____

    _____

    _____ 2

(*c*)   State the term which describes the action of the liver in the breakdown of alcohol.

    _____   1

[Turn over

DO N
WRI
IN T
MAR

Marks

10. The flow diagram below links the structures involved in the blinking reflex response.

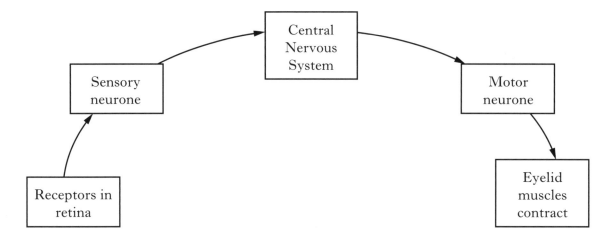

(a) The neural system can show plasticity of response.

Explain this statement with regard to the blinking reflex.

_____

_____ **1**

(b) Describe how the structure of sensory and motor neurones ensures that transmission of impulses is rapid.

_____

_____ **1**

Marks

10. (continued)

(*c*) The diagram below shows the junction between a motor neurone and a muscle fibre.

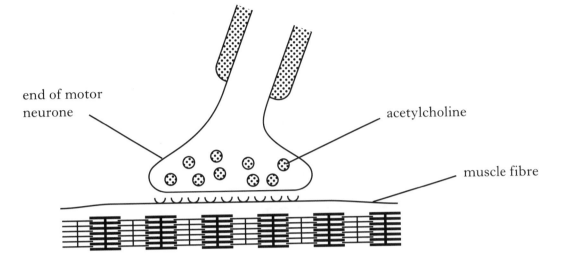

end of motor neurone

acetylcholine

muscle fibre

(i) Describe how impulses pass between the motor neurone and the muscle fibre.

2

(ii) State what happens to acetylcholine after it has carried out its function.

1

[Turn over

Marks

11. A student carried out an investigation to determine the effect an audience has on the performance of a task.

In the investigation, each individual had to move a metal ring along a curved wire, without touching the wire. Whenever the wire was touched a light would come on. The diagram below shows the apparatus used.

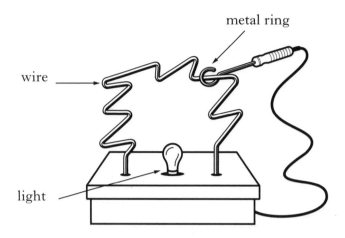

The student started by asking each individual to carry out the task without an audience.

She then asked them to repeat the task with an audience present.

The results of the investigation are shown in the table below.

Individual	Performance (Number of times the ring touched the wire when carrying out the task)	
	Without an audience	With an audience
1	3	3
2	5	2
3	6	3
4	5	0
5	2	3
6	1	1
7	5	3
8	3	1
9	5	0
10	3	2

(a) Calculate the average improvement in performance caused by the presence of an audience.

Space for calculation

_____ 1

DO NOT
WRITE
IN THIS
MARGIN

Marks

11. **(continued)**

(b) State the term which describes the improvement in performance caused by the presence of an audience.

_____   **1**

(c) It is possible that the improvement in performance in this investigation resulted from practice and not the presence of the audience.

Without changing the apparatus, suggest how the design of the investigation could be improved to remove this possibility.

_____

_____

_____   **1**

(d) Describe how this investigation could be redesigned to investigate the effects of practice on performance.

_____

_____

_____   **1**

[Turn over

Marks

12. Three groups of children were shown cards of the following objects.

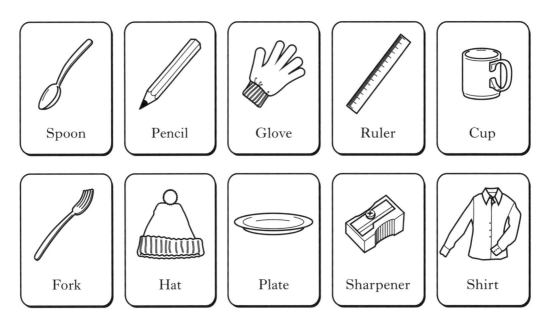

Spoon   Pencil   Glove   Ruler   Cup

Fork   Hat   Plate   Sharpener   Shirt

(a) Each group of children was given a different method to use in order to memorise the objects. The methods used by each group are shown below.

Group 1 — making up a story to include the objects
Group 2 — sorting the objects into related categories
Group 3 — saying the names of the objects to themselves several times

(i) State the term that describes the method used by each group to transfer the objects into long-term memory.

Group 1 _____

Group 2 _____

Group 3 _____   2

(ii) Several days later, the children were asked to recall the list of objects. Suggest an appropriate contextual cue that the children could use.

Explain how this cue would aid their recall.

Contextual cue _____

Explanation _____

_____   1

(b) Most people with Alzheimer's disease would not be able to recall all the objects.

State the area of their brain which is not able to form memories during this task.

_____   1

DO NOT
WRITE
IN THIS
MARGIN

Marks

13. Disease is a major regulatory factor of populations.

(*a*) Human living conditions can influence the spread of disease.

In the table below, list **two** examples of poor living conditions and explain why they could increase the spread of disease.

Example of poor living conditions	*Why it increases the spread of disease*

2

(*b*) Concerns about the MMR vaccine caused the percentage of children in the UK immunised against measles, mumps and rubella to fall below the critical level of 80% between 2000 and 2005. As a result, outbreaks of these viral diseases occurred in various parts of the country.

(i) State what is present in an injection of vaccine.

_____

_____ 1

(ii) Explain how the process of vaccination prevents a child from showing symptoms of mumps during future outbreaks of the disease.

_____

_____

_____ 1

(iii) Suggest why these diseases spread more rapidly when the vaccination level falls below 80%.

_____

_____

_____ 1

(*c*) Another disease that affects humans is tetanus.

Protection against tetanus can be provided actively or passively.

Explain how an individual can be given passive immunity against tetanus.

_____

_____ 1

Marks

14. The graph below shows the changes in atmospheric carbon dioxide measured in a European forest between 2008 and 2013.

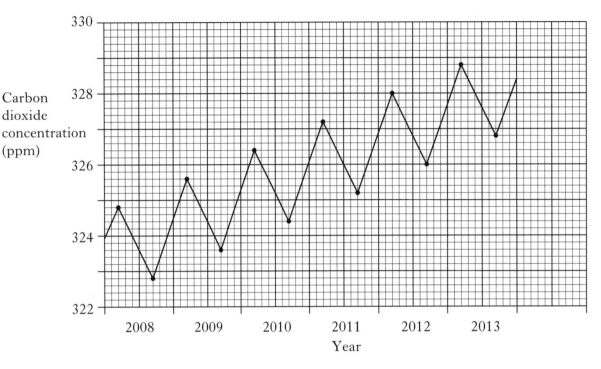

(*a*) (i) State the minimum carbon dioxide concentration recorded in 2010.

_____ ppm   **1**

(ii) Predict the maximum carbon dioxide concentration that would be recorded in 2014.

_____ ppm   **1**

(*b*) Suggest why there is a general upward trend in global atmospheric carbon dioxide concentration.

_____

_____   **1**

(*c*) Carbon dioxide is a greenhouse gas.

Name another greenhouse gas and give a reason why its concentration is increasing in the atmosphere.

Gas_____

Reason_____

_____   **1**

DO NOT
WRITE
IN THIS
MARGIN

SECTION C

Marks

Both questions in this section should be attempted.

Note that each question contains a choice.

Questions 1 and 2 should be attempted on the blank pages which follow.

Supplementary sheets, if required, may be obtained from the Invigilator.

Labelled diagrams may be used where appropriate.

1. Answer **either** A **or** B.

    A   Describe protein synthesis under the following headings:

        (i)   events that occur in the nucleus;   **4**

        (ii) events that occur at a ribosome.   **6**

        (10)

    OR

    B   Describe aerobic respiration under the following headings:

        (i)   events that occur in the matrix of a mitochondrion;   **5**

        (ii) events that occur on the cristae of a mitochondrion.   **5**

        (10)

In question 2, ONE mark is available for coherence and ONE mark is available for relevance.

2. Answer **either** A **or** B.

    A   Discuss the factors that influence the development of human behaviour.   **(10)**

    OR

    B   Discuss ways in which global food supply has been increased to provide for a growing human population.   **(10)**

[END OF QUESTION PAPER]

DO
WR
IN
MAR

SPACE FOR ANSWERS

SPACE FOR ANSWERS

DO N
WRI
IN T
MAR

SPACE FOR ANSWERS

DO NOT
WRITE
IN THIS
MARGIN

SPACE FOR ANSWERS

ADDITIONAL GRAPH FOR QUESTION 2(*d*)(i)

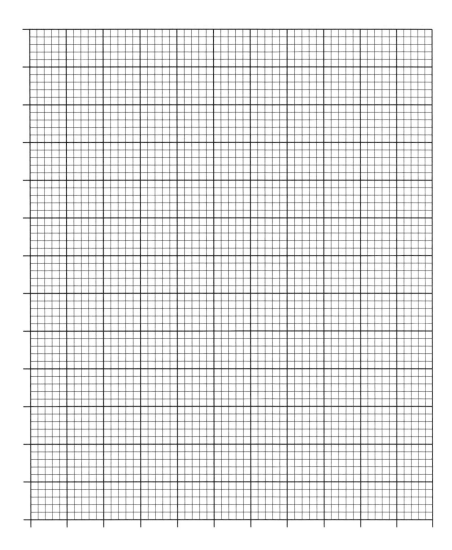

Acknowledgements

Permission has been sought from all relevant copyright holders and Hodder Gibson is grateful for the use of the following:
Image © BrianSM/Shutterstock.com (2013 page 20);
Image © aporokh at gmail dot com/Shutterstock.com (2013 page 20).

HIGHER | ANSWER SECTION

HIGHER HUMAN BIOLOGY
2010

SECTION A

1.	C	16.	D
2.	D	17.	B
3.	D	18.	C
4.	B	19.	A
5.	D	20.	B
6.	A	21.	A
7.	C	22.	B
8.	D	23.	C
9.	C	24.	B
10.	D	25.	C
11.	A	26.	A
12.	A	27.	D
13.	C	28.	D
14.	A	29.	B
15.	B	30.	C

SECTION B

1. (a) Meiosis/meiotic (division)

(b) A = 46   B = 23   C = 23

(c) B has two chromatids/strands and C has one
(chromatid/chromosome/strand) **or**
B is double stranded and C is single stranded

(d) Independent/random assortment and crossing over

(e) Seminiferous tubules

2. (a)

Stage	Name	Location
A	Glycolysis	Cytoplasm
B	Krebs/Tricarboxylic/ Citric acid cycle	Matrix of mitochondrion
C	Cytochrome/ Hydrogen/electron transfer system/chain	Cristae of mitochondrion

(b) Pyruvic acid – 3 (carbons) and citric acid 6 (carbons)

(c) R is NAD and R transports/delivers/carries hydrogen
S is Oxygen and S removes hydrogen/acts as the (final)
hydrogen acceptor/joins with hydrogen to form water

(d)

Situation	Respiratory substrate	Explanation
Prolonged starvation	Protein/ amino acids	Carbohydrates/ glycogen/glucose <u>and</u> fats/lipids have been used up **or** protein is the only (remaining) energy source/ substrate **or** all other substrates/energy sources used up
Towards the end of a marathon race	Fat/fatty acids/ lipids	Carbohydrate/ glycogen/glucose has been used up

3. (a) (i) P = antigen   Q = antibody
(ii) B – lymphocyte
(iii) (A) T-lymphocyte
makes contact with infected cells <u>and</u> destroys
them/breaks them down/perforates membrane.
(B) Macrophage – engulfs/envelops bacteria

(b) (i) **active** and **naturally**
(ii) **active** and **artificially**

(c) Immune system/antibodies attacks body <u>cells</u>
or Immune system recognises body cells/own antigens as
foreign/non-self

4. (a) Lactose can be broken down into <u>two</u>
sugars/monosaccharides/glucose and galactose
or Lactose is built up from <u>two</u> sugars/
monosaccharides/glucose and galactose

(b) *Any two from:*
1. volume of milk
2. volume of enzyme/lactase
3. concentration of enzyme/lactase
4. temperature of the milk/solution
5. age of milk

(c)

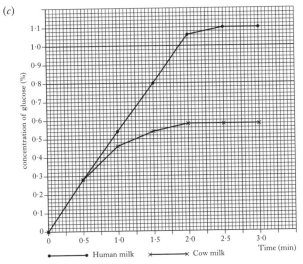

Correct scales and labels on axes
Points correctly plotted and lines drawn going to zero
Lines distinguished from each other (eg key given)

(d) Human milk contains more <u>lactose</u> (than cow's milk)

(e) Lactose/substrate is used up/starts to limit the rate of
reaction

(f) Repeat experiment <u>and</u> calculate an average

(g) (i) An <u>inborn</u> error of metabolism/<u>inborn</u> metabolic disorder/error

(ii) (Blood) glucose levels will remain/stay at normal/constant concentration/does not rise/stays low

5. (a) (i) Prolactin

(ii) Synthesis/production of proteins/antibodies

(b) (i) Colostrum

(ii) Contains <u>more/many</u> antibodies/protein/ vitamin A **or** Contains <u>less</u> fat/lactose/vitamin C **or** Colostrum is more yellow/more watery

(iii) Allows for <u>bonding/attachment</u>

6. (a) Emulsification of <u>fats/lipids/oils</u> **or** Breakdown of <u>fats/lipids/oils</u> to smaller droplets/ globules

(b) Absorbed across/enters <u>villi</u> (of small intestine) Passes into <u>lacteal</u> Transported through <u>lymphatic system/lymph</u> (to bloodstream)

(c)

Substance	Blood vessel	
	Hepatic portal vein	Hepatic vein
Glucose	**Higher**	**Lower**
Urea	**Lower**	**Higher**

(d) (The presence of) valves **or** Large lumen/diameter/bore (reduces resistance to blood flow)

(e) Detoxification

7. (a) (i) 118 beats/min

(ii) 5

(iii) 8.4/8.5/8.6

(b) (i) *Any three from:*
Increased muscle contraction occurs/muscles work harder
This requires more energy/ATP
Not enough oxygen (reaches muscles to release enough energy)/oxygen debt builds up (in muscles)
(More) <u>anaerobic</u> respiration occurs **or**
Pyruvic acid not converted to acetyl CoA/pyruvic acid converted to lactic acid

(ii) Use monitor to) keep pulse rate below/at <u>150 beats/min</u> when running
This will keep <u>lactic acid</u> levels low/at 1.4 mMol/l **or**
This prevents a build up of <u>lactic acid</u>

8. (a) (i) *Any two from:*
High/higher glucose concentration
Large/larger increase in glucose concentration
Glucose concentration decreases slowly/does not return to starting value/norm

(ii) A – Insulin
B – Glucagon

(b) (i) Pituitary (Gland)

(ii) Produce a high volume of urine/increased water loss **or**
Low concentration of urine **or**
Dehydration/thirst/low blood pressure/lower water concentration in blood **or**
Less water <u>reabsorbed</u> (in kidney/back into blood) **or**
No change in permeability of kidney tubules **or**
Cannot control blood water level/concentration

9. (a) (i) Vesicle fuses/joins with membrane <u>and</u> neurotransmitter is released (into synapse/synaptic cleft) **or**
It is released by <u>exocytosis</u> (into synapse/synaptic cleft)
Neurotransmitter <u>diffuses</u> across the synapse **or**
Travels across synapse <u>and</u> attaches to receptor

(ii) Two or more cells/axons/nerve fibres meet one cell/cell Y
More neurotransmitter is released (which stimulates/binds to more receptors) **or**
Threshold is more likely to be reached

(b) (i) Limbic System/hippocampus

(ii) Alzheimer's (disease)

10. (a) Monozygotic twins are <u>genetically</u> identical/share same genes/DNA **or**
<u>Genetic</u> factors can be discounted
Therefore, any difference between them must be due to the <u>environment</u>

(b) (i) Environmental
Little difference exists between the three groups/pairs **or**
A high percentage of adopted (unrelated) pairs have the condition

(ii) Genetic
The more genetic similarity the greater chance of sharing the condition **or**
A very high percentage of monozygotic twins share the condition <u>and</u> a much lower percentage of other/adopted pairs share it

11. (a) Better healthcare/increased use of vaccination/increased use of antibiotics
Example of medical advance (scanners etc)
Example of a social service (eg meals on wheels, sheltered housing)
Improved diet

(b) 1. More young children/0-14 group would be larger
2. Less old people/older groups would be smaller

(c) *Any two from:*
<u>More</u> health provision/doctors/hospitals (for elderly)
<u>More</u> social provision/residential care/pensions (for elderly)
<u>Less</u> school provision/teachers

12. (a) (i) Non-aggressive man and girls

(ii) 1770

(iii) Children will be more aggressive/likely to copy behaviour if they observe an adult of <u>their own gender/sex</u> (being aggressive)

(b) Imitation

(c) Use children who had not seen the recording/adults with the clown

13. (a) Similarity –
Both (nitrogen and phosphorus application rates) peak in <u>1994</u> **or**
Both increase up to <u>1994</u> <u>and</u> both decrease after (1994) **or**
both nitrogen and phosphorus application rates are lower in <u>2006</u> than in <u>1986</u>
Difference –
Nitrogen application rates are <u>always</u> higher than phosphorus application rates **or**
Overall decrease in nitrogen application rate is greater than overall decrease in phosphorus/ nitrogen rate drops faster than phosphorus rate.

(b) 3 : 1

(c) (i) Less algal blooms/less eutrophication/less fertiliser in waterways/less leaching of fertiliser

(ii) Decrease in (crop) yield

Decrease in crop growth/rate of crop growth

14. (a) (i) 0.28

(ii) Erosion/loss of farmland/decreased crop yield/loss of homes/overcrowding/emigration

(b) (i) *Any two from:*

Carbon dioxide/Methane/CFCs/Nitrous oxides/Water vapour

(ii) *Any two from:*

Carbon dioxide – burning fossil fuels/power stations/transportation/deforestation

Methane – rice fields/cattle/landfill sites/melting permafrost

CFCs – aerosols <u>and</u> fridges/freezers

Nitrous oxides – burning fossil fuels <u>and</u> agricultural soil (nitrification and denitrification)

Water – increased evaporation <u>and</u> plane travel

SECTION C

1A (i) **Short term memory**

1. Capacity is around 7 pieces of information (+/- 2)

2. This is called the <u>memory span</u>

3. Held for a (very) short period of time/seconds only/30 seconds

4. Chunking increases memory span/capacity/information held

5. Example of chunking <u>described</u> (not just 'eg phone numbers')

6. <u>Serial position</u> effect named <u>and</u> described (or labelled graph)

7. <u>Encoding</u> named <u>and</u> two methods mentioned (acoustic, semantic, visual, smell, taste, touch)

(ii) **The transfer of information between short and long-term memory**

8. <u>Rehearsal</u> named <u>and</u> described (repetition/rehearsing of items to be memorised)

9. <u>Organisation</u> named <u>and</u> described (putting items into groups or categories)

10. <u>Elaboration</u> named <u>and</u> described (adding meaning to information)

10a. mention of all three terms without description

10b. mention of all three descriptions without terms

11. <u>Retrieval</u> named <u>and</u> described (taking information out of long-term memory)

12. <u>Contextual cues</u> aid retrieval/remembering

13. Example of contextual cue given

14. <u>Description</u> of a memory aid (mnemonics/ mind map)

1B (i) **Chemical use**

1. <u>Fertilisers</u> are used to improve plant growth/provide nutrients for plants

2. <u>Pesticides/insecticides</u> are used to kill/remove pests/insects

3. <u>Herbicides</u> are used to kill/remove weeds

4. Herbicides reduce competition between weeds and crops

5. <u>Fungicides</u> are used to kill fungi/reduce fungal infections

5a. Three terms (-cides) without descriptions

6. <u>Antibiotics/growth hormones</u> improve growth of animals

(ii) **Genetic improvement**

7. Selective breeding (or description)

8. Example of increased yield/increased disease resistance from selective breeding (more grain, more milk etc)

9. Genetic engineering/genetic manipulation/ genetic modification/somatic fusion

10. Definition of genetic engineering as genes being transferred between organisms

11. Result of genetic engineering is increased yield/disease resistance/drought resistance

(iii) **Land use**

12. Deforestation/description of forest removal

13. Marginal land use described/land reclamation/terracing hillsides

14. Irrigation <u>described</u>

15. Removal of hedgerows/creation of large fields/monoculture use

16. Mechanisation/crop rotation linked to more efficient use of land

2A 1. Contraception is prevention of fertilisation/pregnancy

2. Fertile period lasts for a few days around day 14/mid point of menstrual cycle

3. Fertile period can be detected by <u>rise</u> in body temperature

4. Fertile period can be detected by changes in <u>cervical</u> mucus/mucus becomes thinner

5. Contraceptives can be pills/injections/ implants

6. These contain oestrogen/progesterone

7. Pills usually taken for 3 weeks/one pill taken each day

8. Concentration of hormones (in blood) is increased

9. Causes negative feedback effect/inhibitory effect on pituitary gland

10. Reduced production of FSH prevents maturation of ova/eggs

11. Reduced production of LH prevents ovulation

11a. mention of reduced production of FSH–LH without functions

12. (Prolonged/regular) breast feeding/suckling acts as contraceptive

2B 1. Controlled by <u>autonomic nervous system</u>

2. Sympathetic speeds up heart <u>and</u> parasympathetic slows down heart

3. Medulla (oblongata) is control centre (in the brain)

4. Adrenaline speeds up heart rate

5. Pacemaker/SAN <u>in right atrium</u>

6. Pacemaker starts contraction/produces impulses

7. Impulses cause the atria to contract/atrial systole

8. Reaches/stimulates the <u>AVN</u>

9. AVN found at junction of/between atria and ventricles

10. Impulse (from AVN) carried by (conducting) nerves/fibres/bundle of His

11. (Purkinje) fibres/nerves spread out over the ventricles

12. Causes contraction of ventricles/ventricular systole

13. Followed by relaxation/resting/diastolic phase

HIGHER HUMAN BIOLOGY 2011

SECTION A

1.	C	**16.**	B
2.	A	**17.**	A
3.	D	**18.**	C
4.	A	**19.**	B
5.	B	**20.**	C
6.	D	**21.**	D
7.	B	**22.**	A
8.	B	**23.**	B
9.	C	**24.**	D
10.	D	**25.**	D
11.	C	**26.**	C
12.	A	**27.**	A
13.	A	**28.**	B
14.	A	**29.**	D
15.	C	**30.**	D

SECTION B

1. (a) (i) Nucleus
    (ii) U G U   A C U   G U G   C U C
    (iii) 4

   (b) (i) They result in a short/incomplete protein/polypeptide
       or
       The mRNA cannot bind to the ribosome
       or
       They prevent translation/tRNA molecules <u>binding</u> to mRNA
       (ii) The body/immune system/antibodies attacks body <u>cells</u>/own <u>cells</u>
       or
       A disease in which the body/immune system recognises body cells/self antigens as foreign/non-self

2. (a) Phospholipid

   (b) Antigen/antigenic marker/enzyme/receptor

   (c) 30 : 1

   (d) Diffusion

   (e) (i) (The concentration) would become equal/closer
       or
       (The concentration) decreases inside/in the cytoplasm <u>and</u> increases outside/in the plasma
       (ii) No/less ATP/energy production <u>and</u> no/less active transport
       or
       Active transport stops/decreases <u>and</u> diffusion equalises the concentrations
       or
       Respiration is needed to make ATP <u>which</u> is needed for active transport

3. (a) (i) DNA/chromosomes <u>replicate</u>
       or
       Two <u>chromatids</u> are produced (from one chromosome)
       (ii) <u>Homologous</u> chromosomes/pairs separate
       or
       Cells go from <u>diploid</u> to <u>haploid</u>

   (b) (i) Chiasma/chiasmata
       (ii) RT   Rt   rT   rt
       (iii) Independent assortment

   (c) Seminiferous tubules/sperm mother cell

4. (a) (i) 1 – BO
          3 – OO
       (ii) Blood group = AB
       Individual 6 can only pass on allele O <u>to their children and</u> therefore both alleles A and B must have come from person 5 **or**
       She must provide both A and B alleles <u>to her children as</u> her partner has O alleles/is OO **or**
       She produced an A and B blood group <u>child</u> with an OO male.
       (iii) 6

   (b) 1, 3, 6 and 8.

5. (a) (i) C
       (ii) A/B – <u>Graafian</u> follicle
             F – Seminiferous tubule/sperm mother cell
       (iii) Stimulates/promotes/causes/increases <u>sperm production</u>

   (b) (i) Pituitary (gland)
       (ii) Stimulates/causes contraction of the <u>uterus/womb</u>

6. (a) (i) Bowman's capsule
       (ii) Process – ultrafiltration
       Explanation – <u>Blood vessel/arteriole</u> entering is wider than blood vessel leaving
       or
       Blood flows from an <u>artery/arteriole</u> at high pressure

   (b) (i) Proximal convoluted tubule
       (ii) Reabsorption (or description of reabsorption) of glucose/water/salts/amino acids/vitamins/minerals

   (c) (i) Urine solute concentration increases and urine production rate decreases
       (ii) 19 mg/ml
       (iii) 0.34
       (iv) 1600

7. (a) (i) E – pulmonary artery
          F – aorta
       (ii) *Any two from:*
          1 – B has more carbon dioxide
          2 – D has more oxygen/D is oxygenated while B is deoxygenated
          3 – B has more glucose
       (iii) X placed anywhere inside the right atrium/A
       or touching **outer** walls of the right atrium/A
       (iv) Sympathetic increases rate of impulses (from SAN)/heart rate
       Parasympathetic decreases rate of impulses (from SAN)/heart rate

   (b) Supplies the heart (muscle) with oxygen/glucose

8. (a) 199 800

   (b) Not all countries have the same <u>population</u>
       or
       England has a much bigger <u>population</u>
       or
       The <u>population</u> distribution in the (four) <u>countries</u> is not equal

(c) *Any two from:*
1. (Increased spending on) provision of doctors/
   nurses/hospitals/healthcare
2. (Increased spending on) manufacture of insulin/drugs
3. (Increased) education/advertising about diet/exercise
   (and diabetes)
4. (Increased spending on) research into diabetes
5. Reduce advertising of sugar-rich foods

(d) (i) Age – More people <u>consult</u> their doctor about diabetes
         as they get older
         Gender – More males <u>consult</u> their doctor about
         diabetes than females
     (ii) 110
     (iii) 11.76/11.8/12

(e) (i) Pancreas
     (ii) Insulin <u>causes/stimulates</u> the conversion of <u>glucose
           into glycogen</u>

9. (a) (i) X – rehearsal
              Y – retrieval
              Z – encoding
         (ii) Visual/Images/sight <u>and</u> Acoustic/Sounds/audio/
               auditory
               or Any reference to two <u>sensory</u> inputs – smell, taste,
               touch
               or Semantic/Meaning (from LTM) <u>and</u> one sensory
               input.
         (iii) They serve as a reminder to the time/occasion <u>when</u>
               the information was originally experienced/encoded

     (b) The nine digits are divided into groups <u>so</u> there are <u>fewer</u>
          items/chunks to remember.

     (c) (i) Limbic System/hippocampus
          (ii) NMDA

10. (a) 75 <u>and</u> 55

     (b) Similar – cards contain the <u>same words</u>
          Different – words arranged randomly/not organised/not in
          categories

     (c) *Any two from:*
          1. Individuals of a similar <u>age</u> range are in each group
          2. Individuals with similar intelligence/ability
          3. Each group has a similar <u>gender/sex</u> balance
          4. Each group has the <u>same time</u> to write down the words
          5. Investigation carried out in same environmental
             conditions (*eg same room/at same time of day/in same
             temperature/in silence with no distraction*)
          6. Words/cards same size/font/colour

     (d) Organisation (of words into branching diagrams) improves
          their recall/were better remembered

     (e) Repeat the (same) experiment using more/different
          students/more groups of students

     (f) So all students do their best/are more motivated/
          concentrate more <u>due to</u> social facilitation/competition.

     (g) Prediction – Number of words recalled increases
          Explanation – <u>Rehearsal/repetition</u> improves transfer into
          long-term memory (LTM)

11. (a) A – cell body
             B – axon
             C – dendrite

     (b) (i) Acetylcholine <u>and</u> noradrenaline
          (ii) Insufficient secretion/not enough of neurotransmitter
                or
                Threshold level of neurotransmitter not reached

or
Insufficient receptors stimulated
(iii) Protein – <u>Actin</u> and <u>myosin</u>
       Description – They slide between/over/across each
       other

(c) (i) Speeds up (the transmission of nerve impulses)
     (ii) Maturation

12. (a) (i)

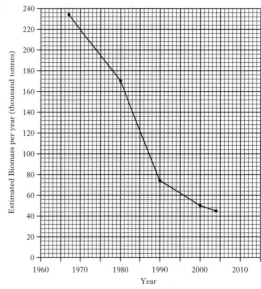

     (ii) 22/23

     (b) (i) 800
          (ii) Less disease/decreased predation/increase in food/
                fishing quotas or bans introduced/mesh size of fishing
                nets increased/reduced demand for herring/less
                competition with cod

     (c) Carrying capacity

SECTION C

1A (i) **The use of language**
        1. Language can be written/spoken/uses symbols (to
           represent information)
        2. Language enables information to be organised (into
           categories/hierarchies)
        3. Language allows the transfer of information/skills/
           instructions/ideas
        4. Language/tone of voice allows communication of
           views/feelings/moods
        5. Language allows learning/intellectual
           development/cultural development
        6. Language allows unique human behaviour/
           distinguishes humans from animals
        7. Language development is dependent on your
           environment/imitation/parents

   (ii) **Non-verbal communication**
        8. Non-verbal communication is important in early life
           <u>before speech possible</u>
        9. It is important in forming <u>bonds/attachment</u>
           between infant and parents
        10. Example described of non-verbal signal by a baby
            <u>and</u> the feeling conveyed eg crying for attention
        11. Non-verbal communication/body language/facial
            expression in adults involves signals that they can be
            <u>unaware</u> that they are giving/<u>subconscious</u> signalling
        12. Non-verbal communication/body language/facial
            expression can aid/replace/ contradict verbal
            communication **or** sign language use by the deaf **or**
            signs used for direction/instruction

13. Non-verbal communication/body language/facial expression can signal <u>attitudes/emotions</u>/feelings

14/15. Two examples of non-verbal communication in <u>adults</u> <u>and</u> the feeling/attitude conveyed eg smiling – pleasure, eye contact – attraction, fidgeting – boredom

1B (i) Deforestation

1. Deforestation involves clearing forests for agriculture/building/transport/raw materials/wood/fuel
2. (Cleared) trees/wood burning releases <u>carbon dioxide</u> (into the atmosphere)
3. More carbon dioxide in atmosphere as less <u>photosynthesis</u> occurs
4. <u>Global warming/Greenhouse effect</u> (as less heat escapes from Earth)
5. Loss of <u>roots</u> (which hold/bind soil) causes <u>erosion/ loss of soil</u>
6. (Increased) flooding/silting of rivers/blockage of irrigation systems
7. Deforestation leads to less rainfall/desertification
8. <u>Loss of habitat</u> so species extinction/reduction in numbers occurs **or** reduction in biodiversity

(ii) Increasing atmospheric methane levels

9. (Increased numbers of) cattle/livestock (to feed population)
10. (Increased) growth of rice/paddy fields (to feed population)
11. (Increased) landfill sites (to deal with waste)
12. Methane produced under <u>anaerobic</u> conditions
13. <u>Bacteria</u> produce methane
14. Methane is a greenhouse gas/causes global warming
15. Methane is produced by <u>biomass</u> burning/burning <u>tropical/rain forests</u> (to clear land for farming)

2A

1. Enzymes are catalysts/speed up metabolism/ chemical reaction/lower activation energy
2. <u>Temperature</u>: enzymes have an optimum temperature/temperature at which they work best/work best at 37°C (*or labelled graph to illustrate*)
3. <u>pH</u>: all enzymes have an optimum pH/pH at which they work best (*or labelled graph to illustrate*)
4. <u>Denaturing</u>: a change occurs in the <u>structure/shape/active site</u> of the enzyme at high temperatures/when the pH changes
5. <u>Inhibitors</u>: slow up/stop enzyme activity
6. <u>Competitive inhibitors</u>: attach to/block the active site so keeping out the substrate molecule **or** inhibitor competes with <u>substrate</u> for active site
7. <u>Non-competitive inhibitors</u>: attach to another part of an enzyme and change the shape of the active site/enzyme (so the substrate molecule does not fit)
8. <u>Substrate concentration</u>: <u>increasing</u> substrate concentration <u>increases</u> activity <u>until</u> a point when activity <u>levels off</u> (*or labelled graph to illustrate*)
9. Explanation that activity levels off when all enzyme active sites are reacting with substrate molecules/enzymes are working at fastest rate possible
10. <u>Enzyme concentration</u>: increasing enzyme concentration <u>increases</u> the rate of reaction (*or labelled graph to illustrate*)
11. Explanation that activity increases due to more <u>active sites</u> being added
12. Vitamins/minerals/cofactors/coenzymes/other enzymes <u>activate</u> enzymes

2B

1. ATP is built up from ADP and phosphate (*or equation*)
2. ATP is produced during <u>glycolysis</u>
3. From the conversion of <u>glucose to pyruvic acid</u>
4. ATP is produced from/by the <u>cytochrome system/electron transport chain</u>
5. This is found/takes place on the <u>cristae of the mitochondrion</u>
6. <u>Hydrogen/electrons passed from carrier to carrier,</u> generating (energy to form) ATP
7. Less ATP produced during glycolysis <u>compared</u> to the cytochrome system
8. During anaerobic respiration/lack of/absence of oxygen <u>two</u> molecules of ATP is produced
9. ATP is broken down into ADP and phosphate <u>releasing energy</u> (*or equation*)
10. ATP is produced as fast as it is used up/remains at a constant level in the body

11/12. Uses of ATP – muscle contraction/phagocytosis/protein **or** chemical synthesis/active transport/nerve impulse transmission/glycolysis/sperm swimming/mitosis **or** meiosis **or** cell division/DNA replication

HIGHER HUMAN BIOLOGY 2012

SECTION A

1.	D	**16.**	C
2.	C	**17.**	B
3.	D	**18.**	B
4.	B	**19.**	A
5.	C	**20.**	B
6.	A	**21.**	B
7.	C	**22.**	C
8.	A	**23.**	A
9.	C	**24.**	D
10.	A	**25.**	D
11.	D	**26.**	D
12.	A	**27.**	C
13.	A	**28.**	B
14.	B	**29.**	D
15.	D	**30.**	B

SECTION B

1. (a) (i) Movement of molecules/substances/ions against a concentration gradient/from low to high concentration/using energy/using ATP

(ii) Contains large numbers of /many mitochondria
or
Mitochondria provide energy/ATP

(iii) Folded/convoluted membrane/surface/provides a large/greater/increased <u>surface area</u>

(b) Proteins

(c) (i)

region	name	respiration stage
X	matrix	Krebs/citric/tricarboxylic acid cycle
Y	cristae	Cytochrome system/oxidative phosphorylation/hydrogen or electron transfer system

(ii) Structure Difference – Mitochondrion would contain fewer folds/cristae
Reason – Less respiration/ATP/energy is required

2. (a) <u>Humoral</u> (response)

(b) (i) B-lymphocyte / plasma cell

(ii) *Any two from:*
Attaches/recognises/identifies/detects the (polio) virus
(Divides to) produce cell Q/ lymphocytes/plasma cells
(Divides to) produce memory cells

(c) To respond <u>quickly</u> to <u>another/a second</u> invasion of a virus/bacterium/pathogen/toxin/antigen

(d) The measles virus carries different <u>antigens</u> (to the polio virus)
or
<u>Antibodies</u> are specific to one virus / polio /antigen
or
The <u>receptor</u> on cell P/the B-lymphocyte/the memory cell does not match the measles virus antigen

(e) (i) <u>Artificial passive</u> (immunity)

(ii) Advantage – provides instant/rapid immunity/protection
Disadvantage – immunity/protection does not last for a long time/ is short-lived/is temporary
or
Memory cells/antibodies are not produced (by body)

3. (a) (i) $R = X^D X^d$ **and** $S = X^D Y$

(ii) 33 / 33·3 / 33⅓

(iii) Son of T = 0 **and** Son of U = 50

(b) (i) Mutation

(ii) Alter/change the sequence/order of <u>bases/nucleotides</u>
or
A specific <u>base/nucleotide</u> change is <u>described</u> (insertion, deletion, inversion, substitution <u>described</u>)

(iii) The protein produced contains an altered <u>sequence/order</u> of <u>amino acids</u>
or
The protein produced contains a <u>different amino acid</u>/is <u>missing</u> an <u>amino acid</u>/has an <u>extra amino acid</u>

(c) <u>Genetic</u> screening/<u>genetic</u> counselling

4. (a) (i) Trypsin/the enzyme digests/breaks down gelatine/protein <u>and</u> releases the (dark) chemicals

(ii) *Any two from:*
Temperature <u>of solution/trypsin</u>
pH
Volume/depth of solution/trypsin
Size/length/area of film
Age/type/thickness of film/thickness of gelatin
Age of trypsin

(iii) Repeat the procedure <u>at each concentration</u> (and then calculate an average)

(iv)

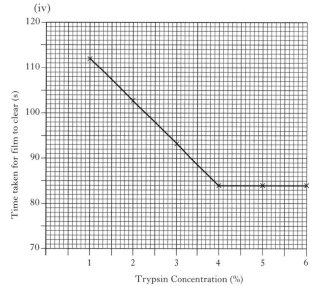

Axes correctly drawn and labelled
Must have trypsin conc (%) **and** time for film to clear (s)
Points correctly plotted and line drawn

(v) There is <u>more</u> trypsin/enzyme (molecules)/active sites to react with the gelatine/substrate/protein

(vi) Surface area of film/size of film/thickness of gelatine is limiting the rate of reaction
or
The size of the film/gelatine is too small to allow all enzyme molecules to react with it
or
The reaction requires a minimum time to occur

(b) (i) The small intestine
    (ii) So that they do not digest the cells/organs/pancreas/glands/tissues <u>that produce them</u>
    (iii) Vitamins/minerals/hydrochloric or stomach acid

5. (a) (i) X = SAN/SA Node/sino-atrial node/pacemaker
        Y = AVN/AV node/atrio-ventricular node
    (ii) The atria contract/atrial systole
    (iii) Arrows must travel <u>down</u> the central wall of the heart from Y and <u>up each</u> side of the ventricles

  (b) (i) Bicuspid/AV/atrio-ventricular
    (ii) Ventricular systole

6. (a) Progesterone

  (b) (i) (Causes the) repair/thickening/proliferation of the endometrium/lining
    (ii) Stimulates/causes LH/FSH release / production

  (c) Progesterone/hormone X remains high/constant/ does not decrease
    or
    Oestrogen remains high/does not decrease during the second half of the cycle/after day 24/25

  (d) (i) P – Graafian follicle   Q – Corpus luteum
    (ii) Ovulation/release of egg from ovary
        or
        surge in LH concentration

7. (a) Breathing rate remains constant <u>and</u> volume of each breath increases
    Breathing rate remains constant at 14 breaths/min
    or
    Volume of each breath increases from 480 to 1240 cm^3

  (b) 18

  (c) 14 000

  (d) (i) 1800 to 1840 <u>cm^3</u> (**units essential**)
    (ii) Lung volume is nearing its maximum capacity
        or
        He is breathing as deeply as possible
        or
        Lungs have a limited capacity/can only hold so much air

  (e) (Carbon dioxide is produced) by <u>respiration/the Krebs Cycle</u> (in body cells)

8. (a) <u>Three arrows drawn</u> – all pointing in the correct direction, ie:
      hepatic artery into the liver
      hepatic portal vein into the liver
      hepatic vein out of the liver

  (b) (i) Bile
    (ii) Function –   Emulsification of lipids/fats
                or
                Emulsification correctly described – breakdown of large fat pieces into fat droplets
        Explanation – This allows <u>enzyme/lipase to speed up</u> the breakdown (of lipids)
                or
                This <u>increases the surface area</u> (of lipids) for <u>enzyme/lipase</u>
                or
        Function –   Neutralisation of stomach acid
                or
                raises pH of intestine
        Explanation – This provides the <u>optimum pH</u> for <u>lipase/enzymes</u>

  (c) Glycogen/Iron/Vitamins (A or D)

9. (a) (The cerebrum) has a convoluted/folded surface/large surface
    This allows for an increased number of cell bodies/cells/neurones

  (b) Transfers/shares information/impulses <u>between</u> the two (cerebral) hemispheres/sides of the brain

  (c) (i) The autonomic (nervous system)
    (ii) Sympathetic speeds it up <u>and</u> parasympathetic slows it down

10. (a) 51 <u>weeks</u> (unit essential)

  (b) 3, 4, 5 and 6

  (c) *Any two from:*
    Genes/inheritance
    Encouragement/attachment
    Diet
    Environment
    One has had an accident
    One has had a disease/has a muscular disease
    One has a slower myelination rate
    One has a (physical) disability
    One had a premature birth

  (d) (i) Maturation
    (ii) Myelination/development of myelin sheath (around nerve fibres)

11. (a) *Any two from:*
    Use people of similar age/gender or gender balance/memory ability or span/use the same number of people/same first language

  (b) <u>Short-term</u> memory/STM holds on average seven/5–9 words/items **or** capacity/span of STM
    or
    <u>Short-term</u> memory/STM can retain words for 30 seconds/a short time **or** duration of STM

  (c) To prevent <u>rehearsal</u> of the words
    or
    To displace/remove the words from <u>short-term memory</u>

  (d) 1. The meaning of words has no effect on their <u>recall/retrieval</u> from <u>short-term memory</u>
     2. Related (meaning) words are harder to <u>recall/retrieve</u> from <u>long-term memory</u> (than unrelated words)
        or
        Unrelated (meaning) words are easier to <u>recall/retrieve</u> from <u>long-term memory</u> (than related words)

12. (a) (i) During Stage 2 it decreases <u>and</u> during Stage 3 it remains constant/steady/level
    (ii) Rapid increase because <u>death rate</u> <u>drops quicker</u> than the <u>birth rate</u>
        It levels off because <u>birth</u> and <u>death rate</u> become similar/equal
    (iii) *Any two from:*
        Increased/improved/better food supply/diet/agriculture
        Increased/improved/better medical provision/vaccination/health care
        Improved sanitation/hygiene/provision of clean drinking water

  (b) (i) Pesticides remove (many) organisms/reduce species diversity/reduce biodiversity
        or
        Removal of pests/animals removes food sources for other species/organisms (further up the food chain)
        or
        Pesticides accumulate/build up along the food chain killing species/animals at the top of the food chain.

(ii) Selective breeding/genetic modification/genetic engineering/genetic manipulation/somatic fusion/crop rotation /irrigation/ mechanisation/ monoculture/ deforestation to <u>create agricultural land</u>/development of marginal land/ terracing / intensive farming

(c) (i) A large/exponential rapid increase in algae

   (ii) *Any four from:*
   1. Decomposition/decay (of dead algae by bacteria)
   2. Increase in numbers of bacteria
   3. Removal/decrease of oxygen (in the water)
   4. Death of other species/fish/invertebrates/animals
   5. Shading effect of algae leads to death of other plants
   6. Toxic algae endangers other animals/man

SECTION C

1A (i) **Natural uptake and release of carbon**
1. (Carbon exists as) carbon dioxide in the atmosphere/air/water
2. <u>Photosynthesis</u> (by plants) takes up CO_2
3. Animals gain carbon by eating
4. CO_2 is released as a result of <u>respiration</u> (by living organisms)
5. <u>Decomposition/decay/breakdown by microbes/bacteria</u> releases methane/CO_2
6. Carbon becomes fossilised/forms fossil fuels/coal/oil/natural gas

(ii) **Disruption of the carbon cycle by human activities**
7. Burning/use of fuels releases carbon/ CO_2 (in the air)
8. <u>Increased population</u> has increased fossil fuel use
9. Industrialisation/transport uses (increased) fossil fuels/releases CO_2
10. <u>Deforestation</u> reduces photosynthesis/reduces CO_2 uptake
11. Increase in CO_2 in air causes <u>global warming/greenhouse effect</u>
12. Methane (CH_4) also causes global warming/is a greenhouse gas
13. Methane production caused by (increased) livestock farming/rice production
14. Domestic waste production/landfill creates methane

1B (i) **The role of neurotransmitters at the synapse**
1. The synapse/synaptic cleft is the junction/gap between neurones/nerve cells*
2. Neurotransmitters are stored in /released from vesicles*
3. Neurotransmitters are released on arrival of impulse
4. Neurotransmitters <u>diffuse</u> across the gap
5. Neurotransmitters bind with/reach <u>receptors</u>*
6. A threshold/minimum number of neurotransmitters is needed (for the impulse to continue)
7. Noradrenaline is removed by <u>reabsorption</u>
8. Acetylcholine is broken down by <u>enzymes/acetylcholinesterase</u>

(ii) **Converging and diverging neural pathways**
9. A converging pathway has several neurones linking to one neurone (if diagram must show direction of impulse)*
10. This increases the neurotransmitter concentration/chances of impulse generation
11. Any example of a converging pathway, eg <u>rods</u> of <u>retina</u>
12. A diverging pathway has one neurone linking to several neurones (if diagram must show direction of impulse)*

13. This means that impulses are sent to several destinations <u>at the same time</u>
14. Any example of a diverging pathway, eg fine motor control in <u>fingers</u> or release of sweat from <u>sweat glands</u>

* Can be given on **labelled** diagram

2A
1. Plasma is the liquid part of the blood
2. (*Any three from:*) named dissolved substances carried – oxygen, carbon dioxide, glucose, amino acids, urea, vitamins, minerals, etc
3. <u>Capillaries</u> have a large surface area/thin walls
4. <u>High pressure</u> (at the arterial end of the capillaries) forces fluid/plasma out
5. <u>Tissue fluid</u> (bathes the cells)
6. Plasma proteins/blood cells do not pass through capillary walls/stay in blood
7. (Dissolved) substances diffuse/move from tissue fluid into body cells
8. Waste products/named example diffuse/move out of the cells
9. <u>Low pressure</u> (at the venous end of the capillary network) allows return of fluid
10. Liquid/water also returns by <u>osmosis</u> (into the plasma)
11. (Excess) tissue fluid enters lymph vessels/lymph
12. This lymph/fluid is carried back to the blood (by lymphatic system)

2B
1. <u>Hypothalamus</u> detects/controls body temperature
2. (Thermo) <u>receptors</u> in the skin/body detect temperature
3. Temperature is maintained by <u>negative feedback</u> (mechanisms)
4. (Increased) sweating results in heat loss by <u>evaporation</u>
5. Increased blood flow to skin/vasodilation causes increased heat loss **or** reduced blood flow to skin/vasoconstriction reduces heat loss
6. <u>Arterioles</u> (not capillaries) constrict/dilate
7. Contraction of hair <u>erector muscles</u> makes hair stand up
8. This traps a layer of air which insulates/reduces heat loss
9. Increased metabolic rate causes heat production **or vice versa**
10. Adrenaline/thyroxine release occurs (when body is cold)
11. Shivering increases/causes heat production by <u>muscles</u>
12. Mechanisms are impaired in older people/undeveloped in infants

HIGHER HUMAN BIOLOGY 2013

SECTION A

1.	A	**16.**	D
2.	B	**17.**	A
3.	D	**18.**	B
4.	D	**19.**	C
5.	B	**20.**	A
6.	A	**21.**	B
7.	A	**22.**	A
8.	B	**23.**	B
9.	C	**24.**	D
10.	D	**25.**	D
11.	C	**26.**	C
12.	C	**27.**	D
13.	C	**28.**	C
14.	B	**29.**	D
15.	B	**30.**	A

SECTION B

1. (a) (i) pH = 8
Temperature = 38
(ii) pH = 6·6 to 8·8
or
2·2
and
Temperature = 20 to 54°C
or
34°C
(iii) High <u>temperatures</u> denature the enzyme / protein
or
High <u>temperatures</u> break (hydrogen) bonds.
The <u>active site</u> is changed / denatured
or
The substrate no longer fits into the <u>active site</u>

(b) (i) (Enzyme) activator / activation / activates
(ii) Trypsin would digest / break down pancreas <u>cells / cells</u> that produce it / <u>cell</u> proteins.
or
Trypsinogen will not digest/break down pancreas <u>cells / cells</u> that produce it / <u>cell</u> proteins.

2. (a) X = amino acids
Y = fatty acids
Z = carbon dioxide

(b) Glycolysis

(c) It / acetyl <u>combines</u> with a 4 carbon compound / intermediate compound /oxaloacetic acid <u>and</u> becomes citric acid / tricarboxylic acid.

(d) Starvation / anorexia
or
When body has used up all carbohydrates <u>and</u> fats.

(e) Name = glycogen
Stored = liver / muscles

3. (a) (i) To prevent multiplication / reproduction / replication of the <u>virus</u>
(ii) To allow recognition by the immune system / lymphocytes
or
So antibodies / memory cells can be produced

(b) X is active and natural
Y is active and artificial

(c) Different strains of flu / the viruses have <u>different</u> antigens / surface proteins / antigenic markers

(d) Attach / bind to <u>infected cells</u> and destroy them.

4. (a) (i) H and h
(ii) A = $X^H Y$ B = $X^H X^h$
(iii) 0   *and*
The only allele she can inherit from her <u>father</u> is dominant / H
or
The <u>father</u> does not have the recessive allele / h / the condition / the haemophilia
or
The <u>father</u> would have to have haemophilia (for the daughter to get it).

(b) (i) Their length / size
or
The position of the centromere
or
Banding pattern (after staining)
(ii) Non-disjunction

5. (a) X = FSH
Y = Interstitial cells

(b) (i) Prostate (gland)
or
Seminal vesicle
(ii) <u>Sugar / glucose / fructose</u> provides energy for <u>sperm</u> (to swim)
or
<u>Prostaglandins</u> stimulate contraction of female reproductive tract / system / cervix / uterus
or
<u>Enzymes</u> keep semen / fluid that the sperm swim in at the correct viscosity / thickness

(c) Sperm mother cells = 100
Mature sperm cells = 50

6. (a) (i) Colostrum
(ii) 1. It contains more/higher concentrations / levels / amounts of IgA / antibodies.
and
2. It contains less / lower concentrations / levels / amounts of lactose.

(b) 460 <u>ml</u>

(c) (i) The <u>volume</u> of the milk produced increased
(ii) 1 : 30

(d) 39·9

7. (a) X = arteriole
Y = capillary

(b) *Any two from:*
Oxygen, glucose, amino acids, fatty acids, glycerol, vitamins, minerals

(c) The <u>muscle cells / muscles</u> started <u>respiring</u> anaerobically / without oxygen.

(d) By the lymphatic system / lymphatic capillaries / lymphatic vessels / lymph.

8. (a) 0·3

(b) (i) 75
(ii) 5250

(c) 1. (Increase is) controlled by the medulla / autonomic nervous system.
2. <u>Sympathetic</u> nervous system affects the <u>SAN</u> / pacemaker.
3. <u>Adrenaline</u> <u>increases</u> heart rate

9. (a) (i) A fall in <u>body</u> temperature below normal / below 37°C / to very cold levels / to low levels / below 35°C / to critical levels.
or
The inability to maintain body temperature <u>up to</u> the normal range / <u>at</u> 37°C .
(ii) Their <u>temperature</u> regulation mechanism / shivering / vasoconstriction is less efficient / slower.
or
Hypothalamus / receptors do not detect <u>temperature</u> changes so quickly / are less efficient at detecting <u>temperature</u> changes
or
They have a slower rate of <u>metabolism</u> / less efficient <u>metabolism</u>
(iii) They have a large / high surface area to volume / mass ratio (so lose more of their heat).

(b) (i) Hypothalamus
(ii) 1. (Heat loss) through <u>evaporation</u> of <u>water/sweat</u> (from skin)
2. (Heat loss) by <u>increased/more</u> <u>blood</u> flowing/diverting to the skin/surface
or
by <u>increased</u> <u>radiation</u> (of heat) from blood / skin / surface

10. (a) Arrow correctly drawn / going left to right

(b) DNA / gene / nucleus codes for <u>neurotransmitter</u> / enzyme which makes/breaks down the <u>neurotransmitter</u>.
or
DNA / gene / nucleus codes for <u>receptors</u>.

(c) Mitochondrion/mitochondria
<u>and</u>
Stores / contains / carries / releases / provides <u>neurotransmitter</u> / <u>acetylcholine / noradrenaline</u>.

(d) (i) Has less / no myelin (sheath)
or
Has fewer / less dendrites / synaptic knobs
(ii) Slower <u>impulses</u> / fewer <u>impulses</u> reach the synaptic cleft
or
<u>Threshold</u> less likely to be reached / less <u>neurotransmitters</u> released into the synaptic cleft
or
Less connections to other nerve cells

11. (a) Corpus callosum
(b) (i) 1. The word key / information from left eye went to the right (cerebral) hemisphere .
2. The right hemisphere controls / moves the left hand (so key is picked up).
3. The word spoon / information from right eye went to the left hemisphere .
4. Information cannot be transferred to the right hemisphere / from the left hemisphere. (so spoon is not picked up)
All four points needed for two marks.
Two or three points needed for one mark.
(ii) Prediction – Spoon
Reason – Spoon / information from the right eye goes to the left (cerebral) hemisphere /side of brain which controls language production / speech.

12. (a) It results in a <u>motor pathway</u> / <u>motor memory</u> / <u>neural pathway</u> / <u>neural circuit</u> / <u>procedural memory</u> being established.

(b) Approximate / improved / good behaviour is <u>rewarded / reinforced / praised</u>.

Only <u>successive / over time improvements</u> are rewarded / reinforced / praised.

(c) (i) Generalisation
(ii) She is <u>persuaded/convinced</u> (by friends / the media / relatives / others).

(d) Name – deindividuation
Cause – Loss of personal identity / sense of individuality.
or
Gain of anonymity / 'facelessness'.

13. (a) (i) Change – deforestation / removal of trees
Explanation - wood is used for building / fuel / raw materials
or
Change – loss of grassland / trees
Explanation – land is used for agriculture / crops / housing / transport
(ii) Addition of sewage / human waste / animal waste /fertilisers <u>leading to</u> pollution / contamination / enrichment / more bacteria / loss of oxygen / algal blooms.
or
Water removal <u>reducing</u> flow / volume / depth.
or
Deforestation <u>causing</u> flooding / silting up.
or
Pesticides / fishing <u>reducing</u> fish population .
or
Washing clothes / people <u>pollute</u> the river with soap / detergents.

(b) Example – Rice production or paddy fields / cattle or livestock farming / landfill / permafrost damage
Effect – Global warming / Greenhouse Effect

(c) Demography / demographic trends

14. (a)

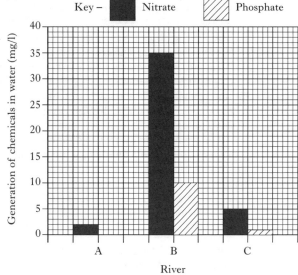

(b) The source of the pollution / contamination is river B / around river B / enters the loch through river B.

(c) *Any two from:*
1. All collected on same day / at same time.
2. Water collected from same depth / distance from bank at each site.
3. Water collected from same distance from loch / up each river.
4. Same volume of water / sample collected.

(d) Take more than one sample from each river.
or
Repeat the procedure with each river.

(e) Take samples at intervals along the length of each river / river B.
or
Take samples from the land / study land use at intervals along the length of each river / river B.

(f) Fertilisers are not added to crops in winter.
or
Decomposition is slower/less bacteria in winter.
or
There is a higher volume of water in the rivers in winter.
or
Frozen soil so no run-off / leaching from land.

(g) *Any two from:*
1. Rapid growth of algae / an algal bloom
2. Increased numbers of bacteria / decomposition
3. Decrease in oxygen concentrations
4. Death of fish / invertebrates / animals / plants
5. Disruption of the food web
6. Reduction in biodiversity.

SECTION C

1A   (i) **Structure of the cell membrane**
   1. Membranes are composed of proteins and lipids arranged in a bilayer / two layers.
   2. Fluid mosaic model
   3. Proteins span membrane and are on the surface of the membrane
   4. Some proteins provide channels / antigens / enzymes / receptors / carriers

   (ii) **Osmotic effects on cells**
   5. Osmosis is the movement/diffusion of water down a concentration gradient.
   6. Water enters cells when in a (more) dilute solution and water leaves cells when in a (more) concentrated solution
   7. Cells should be at the same concentration as surrounding fluid / tissue fluid / plasma / blood

   (iii) **Endocytosis and exocytosis**
   8. Endocytosis is movement of molecules/substances/ materials/chemicals into cell
   9. Membrane/cell folds around / engulfs molecule
   10. Vesicle / vacuole forms
   11. Phagocytosis involves taking in solid particles/ insoluble molecules/bacteria (into the cell)
   12. Pinocytosis involves taking in liquids/antibodies (into the cell)
   13. Exocytosis is movement of molecules/substances/ materials/chemicals out of the cell
   14. Vesicle fuses / joins with membrane and releases contents

1B   (i) **First meiotic division**
   1. Chromosomes consist of two chromatids
   2. Chromosomes arrange themselves into homologous pairs
   3. Crossing over occurs
   4. Chromosomes / chromatids / homologous pairs swap / exchange genes/alleles
   5. At points called chiasmata
   6. Pairs of chromosomes / homologous pairs line up at the equator / middle of the cell
   7. Independent / random assortment / alignment / segregation occurs
   8. Spindle separates homologous chromosomes / chromosome pairs

   (ii) **Second meiotic division**
   9. Chromosomes line up along the equator / middle of the cell
   10. Chromatids are separated (into separate cells)
   11. Four daughter (sex) cells / gametes are formed

   (iii) **Significance of the process**
   12. Provides (genetic) variation
   13. Leads to the production of haploid gametes / cells
   14. The gametes contain half the number of / 23 chromosomes
   15. Leads to establishment of diploid chromosome number / full (chromosome) complement / 46 chromosomes at fertilisation

2A   1. Liver removes oxygen (from the blood) / adds carbon dioxide (to the blood)
   2. Amino acids are broken down / deamination occurs
   3. Urea is released / produced
   4. Hepatic portal vein carries digestion products / glucose / amino acids to liver

5. Insulin stimulates/promotes/causes conversion of glucose to glycogen (not 'converts')
6. <u>Glucagon</u> stimulates conversion of glycogen to glucose
7. Detoxification / removal of toxins (from blood)
8. Example given such as alcohol / drugs
9. Proteins / lipids / cholesterol are <u>added</u> to blood
10. Red blood cells are removed / haemoglobin is broken down
11. Liver stores iron
12. Liver produces /removes / absorbs <u>bilirubin</u>
13. Stores vitamins / vitamin A and D

2B

1. Kidney removes oxygen (from the blood) / adds carbon dioxide (to the blood)
2. <u>Glomerulus</u> is where blood is <u>filtered</u> / <u>ultrafiltration</u> occurs
3. Filtrate / fluid passes into <u>Bowman's capsule</u>.
4. <u>(Red) blood cells</u> / <u>proteins</u> remain in blood / not filtered / too large.
5. Water/glucose/amino acids/vitamins/salts/sodium/ minerals/urea pass through
6. High pressure due to difference in width of (blood) vessels (not capillaries) entering and leaving glomerulus.
7. Glucose is <u>reabsorbed</u> (back into the blood)
8. Reabsorption takes place in <u>proximal convoluted tubule</u>
9. (Most) urea is not <u>reabsorbed</u>
10. Water is reabsorbed / salts are removed in the <u>Loop of Henle</u>
11. ADH increases/causes reabsorption of water / controls the water concentration of the blood / osmoregulation
12. ADH makes collecting duct / kidney tubules more permeable
13. (More) ADH is produced when there is a low water concentration in blood (or vice versa)

HIGHER HUMAN BIOLOGY 2014

SECTION A

1.	A	**16.**	D
2.	C	**17.**	C
3.	A	**18.**	B
4.	D	**19.**	A
5.	B	**20.**	B
6.	A	**21.**	C
7.	D	**22.**	C
8.	B	**23.**	D
9.	D	**24.**	A
10.	B	**25.**	D
11.	C	**26.**	D
12.	A	**27.**	B
13.	C	**28.**	D
14.	D	**29.**	C
15.	B	**30.**	B

SECTION B

1. (*a*) Actin and myosin.

    (*b*) (i) Line goes through **all seven** filaments.
        (ii) They slide over / across / between each other

    (*c*) Only Glycolysis can occur / Cytochrome system cannot occur.
    or
    Glycolysis produces much less ATP / only two ATP molecules.
    There is no <u>oxygen</u> to act as the final hydrogen acceptor / combine with hydrogen to form water.

2. (*a*) Substance – sugar (or named sugar) **or** yeast.
    Reason – (As soon as it is added) the reaction will start.
    or
    So the reaction does not begin (until it is added).

    (*b*) Concentration of yeast.
    Volume / mass of yeast.
    Concentration of sugar solution.
    Volume of sugar solution / mass of sugar
    Concentration of methylene blue dye.
    Volume/number of drops of methylene blue dye.
    Temperature <u>of solutions</u>.
    Type of yeast.

    (*c*) Repeat the investigation using each sugar solution.
    or
    Repeat the investigation and take an average.

    (*d*) (i) Correct scales and labels on axes.
        Plotting points correctly and drawing lines.
        Labelling/distinguishing the <u>three</u> lines.

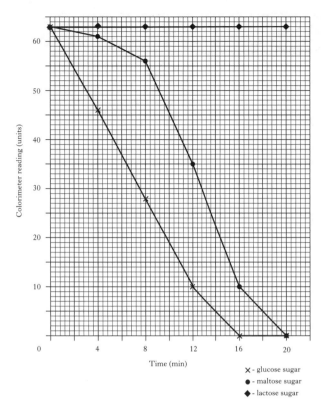

x - glucose sugar
● - maltose sugar
◆ - lactose sugar

(ii) Glucose is the best/preferred <u>respiratory</u> substrate (for yeast).
or
Glucose can be <u>respired</u> fastest/faster than maltose (and lactose)
or
Lactose is not a <u>respiratory</u> substrate (for yeast but the others are).

(e) (i) Maltose has to be digested / broken down before yeast could use it (for respiration).
(ii) The yeast did not contain the enzyme necessary to break down lactose.
or
The yeast was unable to digest / break down lactose.
or
Lactose does not contain glucose.
or
Lactose is not broken down to glucose /respiratory substrates.

3. (a) (i) Macrophage/monocyte/neutrophil.
(ii) Structure Y – lysosome.
Function – Attaches to/fuses with the vacuole/vesicle (membrane) <u>and</u> releases <u>enzymes</u> into it.
(iii) Exocytosis.

(b) <u>B-lymphocytes</u> are stimulated / recognise bacteria / multiply / produce plasma cells / produce antibodies. <u>Antibodies</u> are produced / released which bind / attach to (bacterial) <u>antigens</u>.

4. (a) (i) Individual 3 – X^{d}Y.
Individual 4 – X^{D}X^d.
(ii) The allele is carried on the X chromosome <u>and</u> the father/indiv1 passes the Y chromosome to his son.
or
The allele is carried on the X chromosome and the father/indiv1 does not pass it to son
or
The allele is carried on the X chromosome <u>and</u> the father/indiv1 passes the X chromosome to his daughter.

(iii) 50.

(b) The <u>sequence</u> / <u>order</u> of amino acids is changed (from that point).
or
<u>Different</u> amino acids (in enzyme).
The <u>shape</u> / <u>active site</u> of the enzyme will change.

(c) 250.

5. (a) A – oviduct / fallopian/uterine tube.
B – endometrium / endometrial lining.

(b) FSH – causes growth/development/ maturation (of follicle).
or
(stimulates) release/production of oestrogen.
LH – causes development of / maintains (corpus luteum).
or
(stimulates) release/production of progesterone.

(c) Cleavage.

(d) The zygote develops into two embryos/balls of cells.
or
Two cells divide/split into two embryos/balls of cells
or
One ball of cells divides/splits into two embryos/balls of cells.

6. (a) 120.

(b) Relaxed **AND** relaxed.

(c) Open – semilunar (valve).
Closed – atrioventricular/AV/bicuspid (valve).

(d) <u>Longer time</u> for diastole / between the peaks / for each stage.
or
Peaks further apart.
or
<u>Less frequent</u> peaks / systole.
or
Cardiac cycle takes <u>more time</u> / is longer.

7. (a) (i) 13·8 μl/ml.
(ii) 96·8.

(b) Insulin stimulates the conversion of glucose to <u>glycogen</u>
or
less glucose is stored as <u>glycogen</u>.
This results in glucose being used for respiration / ATP / energy production (in muscle tissue).

(c) (i) 300.
(ii) 29 : 1.
(iii) Volume – increased heart rate / cardiac output / vasodilation (of arterioles / arteries).
Distribution – vasodilation (of arterioles / arteries in muscles).

8. (a) (i) Tissue Fluid.
(ii) It contains no/little protein.

(b) Interstitial cells – testosterone.
Pancreas – insulin / glucagon.
Leg muscle (after a sprint) – lactic acid.

(c) Valves prevent the backflow of lymph.
Contraction / movement of (skeletal) <u>muscles</u>.

9. (a) (i) Q – Hepatic Artery.
R – Hepatic Portal Vein.
(ii) Glucose – R / hepatic portal vein
Urea – P / hepatic vein

(b) *Any two from:*
Iron is stored in the liver / recycled / reused.
Haem is converted to bilirubin / bile / bile pigments

or

Bilirubin is removed in faeces / excreted

or

Bile is stored in gall bladder.
Amino acids are deaminated / used in protein synthesis.

(c) Detoxification.

10. (a) It can be suppressed / resisted / controlled (so that it does not occur all the time).

or

An alternative neural pathway can override the reflex pathway.

or

The brain can be trained / conditioned to stop / ignore the reflex response.

(b) Myelination / presence of the myelin sheath.

(c) (i) Vesicles move to membrane and release acetylcholine / neurotransmitter into the synapse / synaptic cleft.

or

Acetylcholine / neurotransmitter is released by exocytosis into the synapse / synaptic cleft.
Acetylcholine/neurotransmitter combines with/joins receptors (on muscle fibres).

(ii) Broken down/digested/ removed by an enzyme / acetylcholinesterase

11. (a) 2.

(b) Social Facilitation.

(c) *Any one from:*
Repeat the experiment with different individuals who do the task in front of an audience before doing it without an audience.

or

One group performs the task with an audience first while another group performs the task without the audience first.

or

Two groups of similar ability, one of which does the task with the audience while the other does it without the audience.

(d) Individuals should each repeat it more than once with either the audience or without the audience.

12. (a) (i) Group 1 – elaboration (of meaning).
Group 2 – organisation.
Group 3 – rehearsal.

(ii) Contextual cues – same environment / time / seat / location / people / group of children / presenter / clothes worn / scent.
Explanation – It reminds them when the memory was made / encoded.

(b) Limbic System / hippocampus

13. (a) **Condition 1**
Poor sanitation – *Contaminated or dirty drinking/washing water.*
Contaminated drinking/washing water – *contact with bacteria / virus / parasites / specific example – cholera, typhoid, dysentery.*
Sewage not treated – *contaminates drinking water / contact with bacteria / virus / parasites / specific example – cholera, typhoid, dysentery.*

Condition 2
Poor hygiene – *contact with bacteria / virus / contaminated food*

Poor cleanliness of work surfaces – *contaminated food / contact with bacteria / presence of pests.*

Condition 3
Overcrowding – *bacteria can easily pass from person to person / increased chance of contact with bacteria/ fungus / virus*
Lack of ventilation / damp housing – *increased chance of contact with bacteria / fungus / virus*

(b) (i) Harmless / dead / attenuated / weakened microbes / pathogens / bacteria / viruses

or

Damaged viral DNA and intact protein coat/antigen.

(ii) It allows the quick production of antibodies (against it).

(iii) Non-vaccinated people are more likely to get the disease / meet an infected person.

or

Infected people are more likely to spread the disease / meet a non-vaccinated person.

(c) Given / injected with antitoxin / antibodies.

or

Antibodies passed across the placenta / in breast milk / colostrum.

14. (a) (i) 324·4.
(ii) 329·6.

(b) More fossil fuel use

or

Deforestation.

(c) Gas – methane.
Reason – more sewage/landfill/paddy fields / cattle / livestock.
Also accept
CFCs – more aerosols/fridges/freezers.

or

Nitrous oxides – burning more fossil fuels.

or

Water vapour – increased evaporation/plane travel.

SECTION C

1A (i) **Events that occur in the nucleus**
Any four points from the following:
1. DNA unzips/hydrogen bonds break/DNA strands separate.
2. RNA nucleotides pair with DNA bases.
3. Guanine pairs with cytosine, uracil pairs with adenine. (*not base letters*)
4. Sugar phosphate bonds form /sugar phosphate backbone forms.
5. This requires ATP/enzymes / RNA polymerase.
6. mRNA leaves the nucleus.

(ii) **Events that occur in the ribosome**
Any six points from the following:
7. mRNA attaches / moves to the ribosome.
8. tRNA carries amino acid to mRNA /ribosome.
9. Each tRNA molecule is attached to a specific amino acid.
10. tRNA/mRNA has a anticodon/codon of three bases.
11. Anticodon binds to / aligns with codon.
12. Order of codons/bases determines the order of amino acids.
13. Peptide bonds form between amino acids.
14. Ribosome moves along the mRNA strand.
15. Transcription and translation terms used correctly.

1B **(i)** **Events that occur in the matrix of a mitochondrion**

Any five points from the following:

1. The Krebs Cycle/Citric Acid Cycle/TCA Cycle (occurs here).
2. Pyruvic acid enters (the matrix)/ is produced during glycolysis.
3. Pyruvic acid is converted to acetyl-Co A / acetyl compound.
4. Acetyl (-Co A) combines with a 4 carbon compound/oxaloacetic acid to form <u>citric acid</u>.
5. Citric acid is converted back into the 4 carbon compound.
6. Carbon dioxide is released.
7. Hydrogen is picked up by/combines with NAD/coenzyme.

(ii) **Events that occur in the cristae of a mitochondrion**

Any five points from the following:

8. The cytochrome/electron transfer/hydrogen transfer system occurs here.
9. Hydrogen/electrons are passed from <u>NAD</u> / <u>coenzyme</u> to a carrier/hydrogen acceptor/cytochrome.
10. Hydrogen/electrons are passed along a chain of carriers/hydrogen acceptors.
11. <u>Energy</u> is released to make ATP.
12. ATP is generated from ADP and phosphate/Pi.
13. <u>Oxygen</u> acts as the final hydrogen acceptor / combines with hydrogen.
14. Water is formed.
15. 36 ATP (molecules) are made

2A *Any eight points from the following:*

1. <u>Maturation</u> is a sequence of stages in development.
2. An example of maturation showing at least three stages.
3. Determined by development of nervous system/increased myelination.
4. Inheritance / genes affect development.
5. An example of a genetic condition that affects development – PKU/ Huntingdon's chorea/Down's syndrome.
6. <u>Environment</u> effects of friends / peers / family / teacher described
7. <u>Imitation</u> described
8. Reinforcement / shaping / extinction <u>and</u> description
9. Generalisation / discrimination <u>and</u> description
10. Internalisation / identification <u>and</u> description
11. Identical twin studies are useful as they show the effect of the <u>environment</u>.
12. Identical twins are <u>genetically</u> identical.
13. All behaviour is influenced by a <u>combination</u> of environmental and genetic factors.

The coherence and relevance marks are only awarded when at least <u>five marks</u> have been scored from points 1 to 13 and the following criteria are met.

Relevance – A single short reference to an irrelevant point is not penalised but development of the point is penalised. However, two irrelevant points without development are penalised.
For example, mention of <u>two or more</u> of the following will lose this mark:

references to memory/structure of brain

Coherence – Response should contain paragraphs/subheadings, have a logical sequence and be written in sentences (not bullet points).

2B *Any eight points from the folowing:*

Chemical-use

1. <u>Fertiliser</u> use to improve plant growth / yield.
2. <u>Pesticide</u> / <u>insecticide</u> use to kill / reduces damage by pests/insects.

3. Herbicide use to kill weeds/used to reduce competition between weeds and crops.
4. Fungicide use to kill / reduce damage by fungi/fungal infections.

Genetic improvement

5. <u>Selective breeding</u> explained.
6. <u>Example</u> of increased yield from selective breeding, e.g. more grain, more milk.
7. Genetic engineering / genetic manipulation / genetic modification / GM explained in terms of <u>gene</u> transfer / insertion
   or
   Somatic fusion <u>described</u>.
8. Results in faster growth / disease resistance / drought resistance / herbicide resistance (which increases yield)

Land-use

9. Deforestation to create land for crops/farming.
10. Land reclamation / terracing hillsides (to create more farmland)
11. <u>Irrigation</u> <u>described</u>.
12. Removal of hedgerows / creation of large fields / monoculture use.
13. Mechanisation has allowed more efficient use of land
    OR
    example of mechanisation described.

The coherence and relevance marks are only awarded when at least <u>five marks</u> have been scored from points 1 to 13 and the following criteria are met.

Relevance – A single short reference to an irrelevant point is not penalised but development of the point is penalised. However, two irrelevant points without development are penalised.
For example, mention of <u>two or more</u> of the following will lose this mark:

food preferences / over-fishing / disease / desertification.

Coherence – Response should contain paragraphs / subheadings, have a logical sequence and be written in sentences (not bullet points).